GERMAN PHILOSOPHY AND POLITICS

GERMAN PHILOSOPHY AND POLITICS

BY

JOHN DEWEY

 BOOKS FOR LIBRARIES PRESS
FREEPORT, NEW YORK

INTERNATIONAL STANDARD BOOK NUMBER:
0-8369-5552-8

LIBRARY OF CONGRESS CATALOG CARD NUMBER:
77-133520

PRINTED IN THE UNITED STATES OF AMERICA

FOREWORD TO REVISED EDITION

In February, 1915, I was invited to lecture at the University of North Carolina upon the John Calvin Mc-Nair Foundation. The three chapters which now follow the Introductory Chapter were the result. They were published in the same year under the same title as that of the present book. Since the chapters which were written over a quarter of a century ago were evoked by conditions which were manifested in the first World War, they are reprinted without change, save for a few slight verbal corrections.

The new and introductory chapter bears the same relation to the present world war that the earlier ones bore to the conditions which produced the conflict of 1914-1918. They point out lines of ideological continuity which exist between the Third and the Second Reich; but they are particularly concerned to show how modifications of the earlier philosophy came about—modifications so great that in outward form little identity is apparent. The transformation is connected, as I have pointed out, with the fact that actual conditions in Germany had altered so much that Hitler had to reach a stratum of the population, if he was to come to power, which would have remained cold to the ideological approach of Germany's classic philosophy.

Writers born and bred in Germany, notably Karl Mannheim in his *Man and Society in an Age of Reconstruction,* have pointed out the way in which a kind of mass-democratization released irrational elements which have always existed in human nature but which were kept under control, or at least under cover. Hitler obtained mastery in Germany by procuring for these primitive and irrational elements an organized outlet. He first organized them in the National Socialist Party by means of a combination of strict discipline in the Party under autocratic leadership with unregulated and brutal lawlessness to ward off everything outside the Party. Having succeeded in this work, he is endeavoring to repeat the process he carried out within Germany on an international scale. Anyone who will take the trouble to study the means by which Hitler came to power in Germany will have in his hands the key to understanding the present campaign by which he is striving to give Germany the same dominant position in world affairs that the Nazi party obtained within Germany by following his methods. The more extensive and accurate the study, the more complete is the parallelism that will present itself. The method is something new in the world. It creates a totally new situation. It gives the democratic way of life a significance it never had before. Peoples committed to this way of life now have to demonstrate that its method of attaining social unity, both within the nation and between nations, is as superior to the Hitlerian method of violent suppression as the better elements of human nature are superior to the baser elements which Hitler first appealed to and then organized with true German thoroughness.

I add that since the contents of *Mein Kampf* are now widely known, the translations and paraphrases found

in my introductory chapter are drawn from speeches
Hitler made after he wrote that book. Raoul de Roussy
de Sales has edited a large volume of extracts from
speeches made by Hitler between 1922 and 1941 in-
clusive. This work, published under the title *My New
Order*, is invaluable for understanding the policies of
Hitler. I wish to express my gratitude to the publishers,
Reynal and Hitchcock, for permission to quote from it.
I am also indebted to G. P. Putnam's Sons for permission
to quote from Rauschning's *The Voice of Destruction*.

J. D.

New York, N. Y.
July, 1942

CONTENTS

GERMAN PHILOSOPHY AND POLITICS

THE ONE-WORLD
OF HITLER'S
NATIONAL SOCIALISM

INTRODUCTION

History has probably never beheld such a swift and complete reversal of conditions as that which took place in Germany after the close of the first World War. The transformation is so great in quality as well as in quantitative aspects that it raises the question whether the classic philosophy of Germany has any applicability to the Germany of the National Socialist epoch. A plausible case may be made out for the conclusion that the only factor of identity between the philosophy that brought Hitler to power and the philosophies reported upon in the chapters which follow is belief in the intrinsic superiority of the German people and its predestined right to determine the destiny of other nations. Doubts as to the relevance of the older outlook are not decreased when we recall that the man who effected the remarkable change in conditions is a man of slight education, in the school sense of education, who probably has never read a word of Kant, Fichte, or Hegel.

Facts which lie on the surface certainly forbid the attempt to trace *direct* influence of the established philosophical tradition of Germany upon Adolph Hitler's creed. Absence of direct channels of transmission does not, however, do away with the all but incredible one-to-one correspondence that has been proved by events to exist between the terms of the appeal of Hitler and the response aroused in the German people—a correspondence without which Hitler would have remained an obscure agitator with at most a nuisance value. Only a prepared soil and a highly favorable climate of opinion could have brought to fruition the seeds which Hitler sowed. It is reasonable to hold that absence of direct channels of influence but points the more unerringly to a kind of pre-established harmony between the attitudes of belief in which Germans had been indoctrinated and the terms of the Hitlerian appeal:—terms whose adaptation to the state of German mentality must be judged by the triumph they speedily achieved.

It is not surprising that the demonstrated extraordinary success of an obscure man should have convinced Hitler that he was entrusted by God, or Destiny, or Nature (he uses different words at different times) with a mission from on high to awaken the slumbering German genius to consciousness of its own being and its intrinsic strength. Hitler believed or claimed to believe that he was divinely called to evoke what slumbered in German blood. We perhaps have reason for holding that what he attributes to blood and race is in fact a product of culture and cultivation, in the formation of which the classic philosophers were educational forces. Certain it is that the one thing upon which Hitler lays most emphasis is his success in bringing a small party, of which he was at the outset but the seventh member, to power in Germany, in order then to bring the Germany he ruled to a state in which it threatened—and promised—to rule the whole world. Over and over again he cites these facts as proof that he is the divinely appointed incarnation of the true German spirit and blood:—What else, he asks, could account for his and Germany's triumphant rise?

The factor which most effectually conceals the underlying strains of continuity connecting the creed of Hitler with the classic philosophic tradition of Germany is his own extraordinary flexibility in choice and use of means —combined, as he himself has said, with fanatical inflexibility of purpose. Hitler raised opportunism to the point of genius. The fact is familiar to us in the timing which marks his successive moves into surrounding lands. But it is shown equally in the measures taken between 1922 and 1933 by which he came to be undisputed master of his party and by which he made his party the undisputed master of Germany. The contemptuous underestimation of him which prevailed was an important factor in his success. It gave him time and room for the shrewd changes and shifts in manner of appeal by which he won over workingmen, with their millions of party-socialists, bankers and big industrialists, army leaders and old-time Junkers, to his aims and policies.

A less apparent but equally skillful aspect of his genius in opportunism is found in the way in which he borrowed and adapted to his own use all ideas he ran across provided they reinforced any angle or phase of his appeal. I do not think he can be called a disciple, in any literal sense, of Nietzsche, Houston Chamberlain, Treitschke, or Spengler any more than of Kant or Hegel. He showed his sense of timing in the ideas he used as weapons, and he never allowed considerations of logical consistency to keep him from appropriating any idea that would serve him as a weapon. Perhaps he had less use for Spengler than for any of the others mentioned. The idea of "decline of the west" was the offensive opposite of his own plan for its rise to new heights under his leadership. But he certainly derived inspiration from the following words of Spengler: "Money can be overthrown and its power abolished only by blood. Life is alpha and omega. Life and only life, the quality of blood, the triumph of will, counts in history."

"Opportunism" is altogether too weak a word to convey the meaning I want to bring out. If it is the essence of art to conceal its own traces, it is of the essence of the conditions which made Hitler's appeal successful that it aroused hopes and desires that accorded with the basic beliefs of every section of the German people, without display of ideas of an openly philosophical kind. His uncanny insight into the covert wishes and secret ambitions of every group with which he came in contact enabled him to put upon the German people all which the human traffic would bear—"bear" not only in the sense of standing at the time but even more in the sense of upholding and carrying forward.

It is not possible to say too much about the correspondence, the harmony, the co-adaptation of the creed of Hitler and the dominant temper of the Germany to which he appealed; and its existence points to the necessity of considering the attitudes, the habitual beliefs, the acquired ideas of the German people, quite as much as the things Hitler himself has said and done. It is upon the side of infiltration of the teachings of the philosophic representatives of Germany into popular attitudes and habits that we find underlying continuity between them and the powerful components of Hitler's appeal.

That post-war Germany was a defeated and humiliated nation is a well known fact. That this condition of affairs provided the practical basis of Hitler's appeal is also a familiar fact. Germany was down because it was weak; let it become strong and it would rise. This simple consideration is trumpeted forth by Hitler on every conceivable occasion and in every conceivable guise. Germany had a mission in the world to fulfill, and strength, power, was the absolute prerequisite which would enable it to do its bounden duty. Strength was virtue and virtue was power; weakness was, fundamentally, the only vice. Quotations from Hitler's writings and speeches, and information about his deeds, have made his gospel of force, carried to the pitch of fanatical ruthlessness, brutal intimidation, and cruel persecution, a matter of general knowledge. It is also well known that his policy of suppression of every breath of criticism (initiated by use of gangsters to break up public meetings of other parties than his own) developed, when he came into power, into rigid, forceful control of press, pulpit, public assembly, radio, school, and every agency (including whenever possible private conversation) by which opinions are expressed and formed.

There is no doubt about the place occupied in the system of Hitler, in practical action as well as in doctrines preached, of sheer unmitigated force. Hitler has never failed to carry into prompt effect the dictum he uttered in a speech of the year 1922: "The people needs pride and will-power; defiance, hate, and hate and once again hate." To imbue the German people with this attitude was, he asserted, an important part of the "purifying" process the National Socialist Party had to undertake in bringing the German people from weakness to strength. He taught that "will is the one constant factor, the condition of everything else, even of success in war no matter how efficient arms might be." And by will he understands sheer force in action. In a later speech he used such words as these: "Always before God and the world, the stronger has the right to carry through what he wills. The whole world of nature is a mighty struggle between strength and weakness and an eternal victory of the strong over the weak."

Such passages as these can be multiplied indefinitely, and Hitler's conduct has never failed to accord with the beliefs he set forth in his speeches. There is no ground for doubt of the position of the doctrine of sheer force in the scheme of Hitler. It culminates in creation of a political state having absolute authority, since it has monopoly of all the organs of power, physical and cultural; a state whose leaders are moved "by fanatical devotion and ruthless decision" and in which the one virtue of subjects is implicit, loyal obedience. Popular representations of Hitler's creed, however, usually give a false idea of it, and consequently of the cause of the hold gained over the German people. The mistake consists in treating the gospel of force as if it were the whole of his doctrine. Even a nation like Germany in the state of defeat and depression, needs more than fanaticism, brutality, and hysteria (a word Hitler often associates with the fanaticism he commends) in order to transform itself.

Strange as it sounds, Hitler repeatedly stated that the cause of Germany's weakness, the weakness which produced its defeat, was "spiritual" (*geistige*) and that therefore its redemption must also first of all be spiritual. A rebirth of idealistic faith was the primary necessity. In his *Mein Kampf* Hitler along with glorification of force expressly states its subordination (military and economic alike) to ideas and ideals. Without this strand of continuity with the "idealistic" philosophers who were educators of the German people there is no reason to suppose the latter would have responded as it has in fact responded.

In a speech made soon after coming to power (in 1935), Hitler said there were still some even among the Germans themselves who failed to understand the reasons for the existence and for the victory of the National Socialist party. They were the ones who did not know that the German people could be governed only by appeal "to its inner instincts, its conscience," so that the strength of idealism "alone accomplished the acts which have moved the world." The people came to him, he asserted, "because of the command of an inner voice; reason alone would have dissuaded them; overpowering idealistic faith alone gave the word of command."

We do not need to go to the unreasonable extreme of those who have passed over in silence the brutal side of Hitler's philosophy, that of the role accorded sheer force, and who, concentrating upon the "idealistic" aspects of his message, have seen in it the oncoming of the "wave of the future." But unless we are to indulge in serious miscalculation of the sources of his strength in Germany—a miscalculation which will affect injuriously our peace policies—we need to take account of the belief of the German people in the ideal qualities of his work, and give them, as far as they exist, full recognition.

One can hardly use the word *philosophy* in connection with Hitler's outgivings without putting quotation marks around it. Nevertheless, in connection with his emphasis upon the "spiritual" cause of both Germany's weakness and her recovery to strength, he himself does not hesitate to use the word *Weltanschauung*. Not only that, but he says that the absence of a unified *Weltanschauung* was the cause of Germany's defeat while its development is the prerequisite for her recovery. The word, like many German philosophical words, is vaguely ambiguous, and again, like many philosophical terms, owes considerable of its influence to its very vagueness. The usual English translation is "world-outlook," and this translation certainly carries part of its significa- tion. But it may also be translated "world-intuition." It is characteristic of German philosophical procedure to hold that a look "without" must be based upon a prior look "within." Intuition is in philosophical discourse a method of looking "within" which reveals principles that are first and ultimate truths in spite of their hazy character.

In any case, Hitler has a truly Germanic devotion to a *Weltanschauung*. One of the most serious charges he brought against other political parties while he was striving to bring his own party to power was that at their gatherings no problems of *Weltanschauung* were ever brought up for discussion. A speech that he made to a group of industrialists shortly before coming to power, in 1932, is of first rate importance in understanding the "idealistic" phase of Naziism. It is matter of common knowledge that Hitler was given to attributing the de- feat of Germany in 1918 to a "stab in the back," he having regarded the German army as unconquerable till almost the end. This notion served him well for ordinary popular propaganda purposes. But it is far from expressing his actual explanation of the cause of Germany's defeat. In the address just mentioned (more reasoned and less purely emotional in tone than most of his speeches) he expressly said that it is a mistake to regard the Versailles Treaty as the source of the evils from which Germany was suffering. "I am bound to assert," he went on to say, "that if I am to hold the belief that the German people can exercise an influence in changing these evil conditions, there must have been responsibility within Germany itself for what happened." Logically enough, he held that if the cause for the evil state of the country was external, then the remedy must also come from outside. If cure and redemption could be effected from within, then there was also responsibility from within for Germany's weak and humiliated state.

"They are wrong," he said, "who seek the cause of Germany's distress in externals. Our position is certainly the result not merely of external events but also of our internal, I may almost say, aberration of spirit, our internal division, our own collapse." He then repudiated the idea that the purely "spiritual" side of the catastrophe Germany had undergone could be overlooked, and went on to repeat his protest against "those who claim that the Treaty of Versailles is the cause of our misfortunes." For that Treaty is only *the consequence* of our own slow inner confusion and aberration of mind." Having supplemented this assertion with a corresponding one that only a change in the *Weltanschauung* of the German people will restore Germany to unity and strength, he went on to explain, on historic grounds, the cause of what he repeatedly calls "inner division," "inner conflict," "inner aberration," "spiritual collapse." *

His explanation of the lapse of Germany and the means of its recovery is as follows: "Germany once had a unified world-outlook. Accordingly it possessed the conditions required for large-scale organization, community of religion being the unifying principle. When the rise of Protestantism shattered this basis, the strength of the nation turned from external to internal conflicts, *since the very nature of man forces him by inner necessity to seek for a foundation in a common world-intuition* (or outlook). Otherwise man's nature is split into two, and falling into chaos is unable to turn its force outwards." And just because Germany had failed to achieve a new spiritual unity, "its force turned inwards and was internally absorbed and exhausted." Its preoccupations with its own "internal tensions" rendered it "unresponsive to external events of world-wide significance."

I think we are justified in regarding this account as a confirmation of what I said over twenty-five years ago about the "two-world scheme" of German culture. As has been frequently pointed out, in the absence of any-

* The cloudiness which adds emotional force to many German words is evident in the word *geistige,* here translated *spiritual.* It has the ordinary meaning of *mental,* psychological, and also bears the highly honorific significance many persons find in whatever is labeled "spiritual."

thing comparable to the French Revolution, Germany's "revolution" took place in ideas isolated from habits and institutions in action. Hence Hitler's conclusion as to the sole method by which Germany can recover the unity which is a condition of both domestic and international power. "Unless Germany can master its internal division in world-outlooks (or world-intuitions), it can do nothing to arrest the decline of the German people. . . . We are not the victims of treaties, but the treaties are the consequence of our own mistakes, and if I wish to better the situation I must first change the values of the nation." Hence the address closed with an appeal to the latent idealism of the nation, in which "material," that is, economic, interests are specifically set in opposition to higher "spiritual" interests. Dependence upon the former only leads to further dissipation of the inner spirit from which alone will proceed a unified world-outlook and hence strength. "The more you bring the people back, on the other hand, into the sphere of faith, of ideals, the more it will cease to regard material distress as the one thing which counts." For, he goes on to ask, did not the German people once wage wars for a hundred and fifty years "for religion, for an ideal, for a conviction, without a trace of an ounce of material interest?" And his final word is that when the whole German people has the same faith in its national vocation that has moved the storm-troopers to make their sacrificial efforts (including use of violence on the streets and in the meetings of their party-opponents) the position of

Germany in the world will be very different from what it has been. In short, it was Hitler's mission to overcome that division between the "inner" and the "outer," the ideal and the actual, between spiritual faith and the hard realities of action which had constituted "The Two Worlds of Germany," and for this reason I have felt justified in entitling this chapter "The One-World of Hitler's Germany."

A Berlin professor who left Germany because of opposition to its policies in the first World War, wrote in 1917 the following words under the caption *Philosophy as a Smoke-screen:* "Because of the strong religious bent in Germany, the Renaissance passed off there in religious disputes. The humanists properly so-called never had much influence there.... Men were so taken up with religious liberty they forgot there was such a thing as civil liberty.... Above all, Germany got into the habit of considering the world on which she depended as something far away, above the clouds, and anything 'on this side' or 'here below' as of small moment.... What the German genius needed was that in the free 'world of thought' each person be a law unto himself, while in the actual world he was forced to bow the knee to his superiors." Up to a certain point, there is here the same diagnosis of the source of Germany's troubles as that given by Hitler. Moreover, the writer went on: "The pleasing saying, 'Well, if you won't be my brother, I'll bash your head in,' has become a German proverb. And the German thinks this is the formula by which he can redeem the world.... A Frenchman will never understand this. He is too frivolous and materialistic.* He thinks a dead man is just a dead man, an asphyxiating bomb just an asphyxiating bomb. But the German knows that behind both there lurks something else—an idea. ... Ideas lurking behind things are the excuse for everything, and behind the bombs every German seeks and finds what he wants to find. The Christian finds his God, the philosopher his Kant, the philanthropist his love of humanity, and the Philistine citizen finds universal order."

It will be recalled that Hegel attacked the Kantian separation of what is and what ought to be, of the actual and ideal. He declared that what is actual is the rational and what is rational becomes in virtue of its own activity the actual. But in his dialectic scheme, knowledge of their identity exists only in philosophy as the ultimate manifestation of Absolute Spirit. Any outward manifestation of the identity has to be left to the majestic onward procession of that spirit. Hitler's philosophy, or world-outlook, is that the identity of the ideal with hard fact may be effected here and now, by means of combining faith in the ideal to which destiny has called the German people with force which is thoroughly organized to control every aspect of life, economic, cultural, artistic, educational, as well as military and political.

I shall not multiply quotations of passages in which Hitler insists that his success in transformation of the

---

* It is possible the author came from the Rhineland, whose culture has long been as much French as German.

German people from a weak, divided, and humiliated people to one which is strong, proud, and united springs from the fact that he was the one who understood their latent idealism and knew how to rouse it into action. His policies of "coordination," of totalitarianism, represent his "ideal" of social unification put into thoroughgoing practical operation. In Hitler's own words: "In place of a great number of parties, social ranks, and societies, a single community has arisen. You have sacrificed your parties, societies, associations. But you have obtained in return a great and strong Reich." Abolition of trades unions, of federated states, of *Staende,* ranks and "classes," and of diverse political parties, with the intention of doing away ultimately with differences of religious denominations and organizations; control of schools, press, radio, public and private gatherings: all these things are in the interest of the "ideal" of a community having "inner spiritual" unity and hence strong. They are but the special means by which Hitler did away with the conflict and laceration he attributed to acceptance of the two-world scheme.

A declaration he has issued since the war began says that the "ideal" of the nations against which Germany wars is "struggle for wealth, for capital, for family possessions, for personal egoism"—in short, for unmitigated "materialistic" supremacy of a separate "class" cloaked under a pretended regard for individual liberty. These other nations, he said, war on peaceful Germany because they hate its ideal of complete inner spiritual unity. Germany, on the other hand, is engaged in creating a world of complete mutuality, "a world of mutual work, mutual effort, mutual cares and mutual duties." In this process, "our tasks help bring our people closer and closer together and to create an ever more genuine community." And, as if moved by an inner urgent necessity for making his philosophy of the union of idealism and ruthless force complete, he added, "If there are those who are unwilling to cooperate, we shall give them a state funeral." The consistency of his policy is exhibited in the funerals he is giving the persons in occupied countries who decline to "cooperate."

There are those who are content to define the principle at stake in the struggle of democracy against authoritarianism as respect for personality in the abstract, that is, without regard to concrete social context, and, indeed, as if the bare principle of a personal self automatically produced its own proper social context. They will be surprised to discover that no one has been more ardent in profession of reverence for "personality" than Hitler himself. For example, he has said that "in periods of national decline two closely related factors appear. One of them is the substitution for the idea of the value of personality of a leveling idea of the supremacy of mere numbers—democracy. The other is negation of the value of a Folk; that is, the denial of differences in the inborn capacities and the achievements of different peoples." Again, "it is absurd to recognize the authority of the principle of personality in economic life and deny it in the political domain. I am bound to put the authority of personality in the forefront." Again, "there are two diametrically opposed principles: the principle of democracy, which, when allowed to have practical effect, is a principle of destruction, and the principle of personality, which is the principle of achievement."

I have no desire to interpret these professions as yielding even a verbal deference to the Kantian principle of personality—as an "end in itself." The authority which Hitler gives to personality is that of active or vital energy; the kind of brutal force exhibited in his own career and in the sub-leaders who rallied about him. But the passages should make clear the emptiness of formal philosophical and theological assertion of the supreme value of "personality," exactly as other utterances make evident the barrenness, combined with threat of social harm, of formal proclamations of idealism. To healthy common sense, an "ideal" has meaning when it is taken as something to guide effort in production of future concrete changes in the existing state of affairs. In the two-world scheme of German philosophy, the ideal was the future brought into the present in the form of a remote but overarching heavenly sky—cloudy but still unutterably sublime. With Hitler the ideal became creation of a completely unified "community" by means of force. Empty, formal use of *ideals* and *personality* is not confined to German philosophy. It has found lodgment in the teaching of philosophy in this country and Great Britain. Just as Hitler could boast, with formal correctness, that he brought National Socialism to power under the form of constitutionality, so idealism and personality separated from empirical analysis and experimental utilization of concrete social situations are worse than vague mouthings. They stand for "realities," but these realities are the plans and desires of those who wish to gain control, under the alleged cloak of high ends, of the activities of other human beings. Hitler's success within Germany and the threat to the peoples of the whole world that success has produced is a tragic warning of the danger that attends belief in abstract absolute "ideals."

I turn now to a summary statement of the main components of the philosophy of social unity constituting the creed of National Socialism. Hitler outlined the creed in a speech he made soon after coming to political power (in 1934), and briefly repeated its main points in 1941. The latter can be stated, accordingly, in a paraphrase of his own words. Rallying and unifying the idealism of Germany is the supreme need. This idealism was divided between two camps which opposed one another and which had therefore to be welded together into unity. The masses, the workers, were wedded to socialism. They perhaps did not have definite ideas of just what it signified but it presented to them a necessary and fixed goal. Over against this large group stood a smaller group devoted to the ideal of nationalism. The split was serious because the first and larger group represented the workers, the hand, the productive agency of the nation, while the nationalists represented its brain. The strength and the promise of triumph of Hitler came from the fact that he first, and alone, saw the underlying identity of the two ideals. "The purest form of socialism signifies the conscious elevation of the claims and interests of the life of the people over the interests and claims of the individual." On the other side, "the highest form of nationalism finds its expression only in the unconditional devotion of the individual to the people." In short, true socialism and true nationalism are manifestations of the same ultimate ideal, approached and viewed from its two ends. What one side saw as the superior claim of society, the other side saw as the subordination and devotion of the individual to society. In spite, however, of their intrinsic correspondence, "the task of immeasurable difficulty lying before the Party is translation of recognition of the identity from the world of ideals, of abstract thought, into the domain of hard actualities."

Looking back upon the work of the Party from the vantage point of 1941, he said that so much had been accomplished in overcoming the separation between socialism and nationalism and in effecting the necessary translation into hard fact of their inner kinship, that "today the evolution of the national state is looked upon as a matter of course. In 1918-19 it was looked upon as the figment of a diseased imagination." Then he went on to say: "The ideology of National Socialism represents the conquest of individualism—not in the sense of curtailing individual faculties or paralyzing individual initiative but in the sense of setting the interests of the community above the liberty and initiative of the individual"—the interests of the community in question being of course those of the particular "community" set up by Hitler himself.

There is one important matter in which Hitler's National Socialism represents a break with the orthodox German tradition of political philosophy. Contrary to what is often said, Hitler did not indulge in deification of the State or political organization. What he calls *society*, understood in terms of the people or *volkische* nation, is supreme; the state is reduced, in the theory of National Socialism, to an organ, although an indispensable one, of promoting the security and well-being of the community. At the outset, he could hardly have had any other idea, since he was engaged in a deliberate attempt to overthrow the existing state because it had failed utterly to perform its social function. But as time went on he saw himself more and more as the divinely commissioned representative of the people, of the national community which the government or state he created was bound to serve. It was also much simpler to connect his theory of blood and race with a quasi-mystical notion of the people than with the activities of the state, which are often felt as a burden, as in having to pay taxes.

Hitler also made a change of an extraordinary character in the theory of socialism. Previous creeds that called themselves socialistic attached primary importance to economic factors, no matter what brand of socialism they presented. Hitler comes out flatly for subordination of economic interests and affairs. Work,

productive work put forth in behalf of the community—
the Hitlerian community, of course—is the sole economic factor of importance. To it, all technical economic
questions and problems are completely subordinate; and
in no affair has Hitler displayed his opportunism on
larger scale or with more immediate success than in
his manipulation of capitalists and laborers. Rauschning's statement that Hitler looked upon socialization of
banks, factories, this and that industry, and of private
property as trifling matters, since the one thing of importance is the socialization of human beings, is in line
with the tenor of Hitler's public speeches, although it is
franker in tone than those he made in appealing to
socialist workingmen.

Except when used in the service of national unity, economic activities are external and "materialistic." There
is no reason for supposing that his attack upon Marxist
Bolshevism on this score is not sincere. It was a factor
in his success in converting millions of socialist voters
to his cause. More important with respect to this latter
matter, however, is his subordination of the economic,
given the existing condition of Germany, to development of a powerful government and powerful army.
In his own words, "There can be no economic life
unless behind economic activity there stands the determined political will of the nation ready to strike and
to strike hard." Not even agriculture could be revived
without a prior revival of Germany as a political power.
Foreign trade could be developed only by the same
means. Even with respect to an "internal market, the

problem of the Life-space (*Lebensraum*) of Germany must first be solved by making Germany into a political power factor."

As a means of reaching depressed laborers and the millions of unemployed, the appeal of the communist party to internationalism was indeed theoretical, pale, and remote compared to what Hitler told them—making his word good in his "guns before butter" war economy —he could do if they would assist in building up a powerful German political nationalist state. Present day communists seem to have learned the lesson, possibly more from the example of Stalin in converting the U.S.S.R. from international socialism into a highly nationalistic state—which foolish liberals often take to be a move to the return of capitalistic economy. At all events, the communist party in the United States is quite willing to subordinate distinctively American interests to those of a foreign country which they hold up as a concrete example of a "socialist" state.

The distinctive feature of the ideal Folk-society is that its unity springs ultimately from blood or race. One may read everything Hitler has said and be none the wiser as to what he understands by race. According to good authority, Hitler once retorted impatiently to a critic that he knew the scientific facts about the composite racial structure of Germany as well as anyone. Certain it is that he employs "blood, race, and soil" in a mystical sense, if one defines "mystical" to mean the complete submergence of fact and idea in an overpowering emotion supposed to reveal higher truth than cold intelligence can compass. The following quotation gives a partial idea of the role of blood and race in his appeal. "First of all stands the inner value of a people which is transmitted through the generations, a value which suffers change when the Folk who is the custodian of the value changes its inner blood-conditioned composition. Traits of character are bound to recur as long as the nature of a people, its blood-conditioned state, does not alter. This value, not to be destroyed without a change in blood substance, *is the chief source of all hope for revival of our people.* Otherwise the mystic hope of millions for a new Germany would be incomprehensible."

Scientific facts about race were as nothing in comparison with a simple, easily grasped, symbol which could be used as a weapon in an emotional appeal to fanatical action. Hitler's contempt for intellectual measures and for science, except when used as an effective technical instrument in propaganda, are the obverse side of his belief in the power of emotion to reach the masses, and of his conviction that when "intellectuals" are emotionally stirred they fade into the mass. For it is characteristic of intense emotion to rule out discrimination; emotion is an all or none state. We fear and hate all over; the emotions are inherently totalitarian. When they are once kept excited they control belief and every semblance of intellectual operation. Indifference, apathy, Hitler called his chief foe; excitement, and always some new source of excitement, is the consistent quality in his inconsistent policies. Since emotion is total, it knows only black and white, not intermediate shades. Hence the ideal value of Germanic blood needed for effective presentation an extreme and wholly dark opposite.

There is, accordingly, good reason to believe the report that Hitler once said that if the Jews were destroyed, it would be necessary to invent them. Just as he always presented the mildly socialist regime he was trying to overthrow as if it were the most extreme and dangerous Marxist communism, and just as communists represented social democrats as the social fascist traitors who were the worst foes of socialism, so in the face of all facts he represented the political parties of Germany as agents of the overlordship of international Judaism. His extreme flight and extreme success was his persuasion of multitudes that international finance-capitalism and the communism that was engaged in trying to overthrow capitalism were but two wings of the same army of destruction. Skillful emotional manipulation of symbols probably reached its climax for long ages in Hitler. If it is true, as is sometimes asserted, that he is himself pathological, it is certain that, in the phrase of the street, he is "crazy like a fox," since his own emotional disturbances, if they are there, are of a kind which enable him to arouse similar disturbances in others. As he says of his own teachings, "what the intellect of the intellectual could not see, was immediately grasped by the soul, the heart, the instinct, of simple primitive men." For good measure, he then added that the task of the education of the future is "to grasp the unity of feeling and intellect and return consciously to primitive instinct."

Blood, race, instinct, passion, in the vocabulary of
Hitler, are names for life, for the vital; and they are
a name for what move men to act *en masse*; leaders
above meanwhile exercising with consummate skill the
most approved methods of organization and control.
The mass is not a new phenomenon. Neither is the authoritarian leader. What is new is a mass which is not
a mere amorphous crowd but in which the most extraor-
dinarily effective skill in every kind of organized effort
is combined with the psychology of the crowd. There is
nothing in the career of National Socialism which requires any change in the sentence of the next chapter,
written over twenty-five years ago: "The chief mark of
distinctively German civilization is its combination of
self-conscious idealism with unsurpassed technical efficiency and organization." Only the locus of the "idealism" and the agents of its organization have altered.

That the content which fills and gives toughness to
the idealism has moved from the intellectual (or quasi-
intellectual) to the emotional and passionately impetuous, without losing its combination with technical
efficiency and organization, is indeed new. It is the
difference which has given victory in Germany to the
ideology of Hitler. The transformation, it may be said
with a large measure of truth, was anticipated by Heine
in 1833. I quote again a passage cited in the second
chapter of my original text. After saying that there will
first be a time in which Germans will occupy themselves

with systems of philosophy and that upon completion of
this period a political revolution will follow, he goes on,
"most to be feared are the philosophers of nature were
they actively to mingle. .... The Philosopher of Nature
will be terrible in that he has allied himself with the
primitive powers of nature, in that he can conjure up the
demoniac forces of German pantheism and having done
so, aroused that ancient Germanic eagerness which combats for the joy of the combat itself. . . . Smile not at my
counsel as at the counsel of a dreamer. . . . The thought
precedes the deed as the lightning the thunder. . . . The
hour will come."

It had not come in 1914. At that time there did not
seem to be any likelihood that it would ever come. As
far as Heine had the philosophy of Schelling in mind,
in that particular form, the hour has not come now,
Hitler is doubtless innocent of any knowledge of Schelling. But the spirit of the remark is incarnate in the
teachings and the actions of Hitler. The writings of
Richard Wagner, in his return to primitive Teutonic
mythology, probably have had more influence in giving
shape to Hitler's hopes and ambitions than that of any
other person. At all events, the saying of Hitler, reported by Rauschning, about the coming revival of the
early nature worship of the German people reads like
an almost literal reminiscence of the prophetic vision
of Heine. For after Rauschning had said that the peasants of his district retained below the surface of Christianity beliefs inherited from olden times, Hitler replied,
"That's what I'm counting upon. Our peasants have not

forgotten their true religion. It is merely covered over.
... They will be told what the Christian Church has de-
prived them of—the whole secret knowledge of nature,
of the divine, the shapeless, the demonic."

We do not, however, need to depend upon this remark, nor yet upon Hitler's practical attempts to weaken
the hold of the Lutheran and the Catholic churches, nor
yet upon his coquettings with the ideas put forth by
Rosenberg as to the necessity of a return to primitive
Germanic gods and cults. The idea of a "religion rooted
in nature and blood" (to use Hitler's words) is the only
idea consonant with his whole appeal and with his
efforts to give his National Socialism the emotional intensity, the symbols and the rites of a religion. There is
more truth than appears on the surface in the comparison that has been suggested between Mohammed and
Hitler in creation and propagation of a new and fanatical religion.

Hitler's whole philosophy of "blood and soil," the
passion of his struggle for recovery of every one of German origin in the new community of Germans, his passionate struggle for new lands for Germans to settle
and make their home, spring from his passionate faith
in what he calls "nature." Such statements as these are
typical of his appeal. He ascribed the rebirth of Germany to its response to the appeal he made in behalf of
"the primacy of the eternal values of blood and soil
*which have been raised to the level of the governing
principles of our life*." And again he said, "Our worship

is exclusively cultivation of that which is natural, *because what is natural is the God-willed.*"

It is in this context that we have to understand Hitler's fervent belief that he is the Messiah commissioned to found a "new order" not only for Germany but for the whole earth. The values he calls "historic" are now old to the point of senility; they are artificial, lacking all support in "nature." They are to be replaced by biological values, by those of blood; that is, of life-force. His constant depreciation of "intellect," his assertion that the Germans were cultivated in excess, his reiterated appeal to raw primitive instincts, to the impetuous and unreflective, his supreme confidence in his own supreme leadership, are all of them aspects of his philosophy of nature and the natural—as he conceived them.

To win over captains of industry and socialist workingmen (including abolition of their unions), peasants and Junkers, the old aristocracy and gangster upstarts, strong nationalists and the states-rights adherents of federated states, required a world-outlook that cut below the "intellectualism" of the traditional philosophy of Germany. "Reason" had to be identified with "the most primitive manifestations of Nature." The earlier appeal was to an elite; as long as an elite ruled a powerful and growing Germany it sufficed. But with the defeat and humiliation of Germany, power to rule was passing from the elite. It was the genius of Hitler to grasp that fact. Commentators upon the German scene, German born and bred, have noted that there are certain general industrial and political tendencies which are breaking down class distinctions and creating a new force, that of a more or less amorphous mass. The depression of Germany, combined with traditional political ineptness of the German populace in political matters, and with the abstaining remoteness of the scientifically educated part of the population from political life, tremendously accentuated this phenomenon in Germany. As events have demonstrated, it became, under the skilled manipulations of Hitler, the decisive factor. An inverted democracy with authoritarian absolute leadership at the apex and the disciplined obedient mass at the base, with a hierarchical order of intervening sub-leaders, constitute the political state of Nazi Germany. It is an "inverted democracy" in which place and rank are made dependent upon manifestation of fanatic zeal and resolute energy in command and obedience rather than upon the many feudal inheritances Germany had not thrown off. Exhibition of zeal, devotion and fanaticism is what Hitler understands by "the authority of personality," which in his creed is an expression of the intensity attained in different human beings by blood or natural life-force.

The change from the primacy of *Innerlichkeit* to primacy of action is not what it seems to be upon the surface. What is more "inner" than "blood," and what is more internal and intrinsic and the same time more urgent for utterance than the impulses and passions to which Hitler successfully addressed his appeal? There is even more continuity between this appeal and the political philosophy and the philosophy of history of

Hegel than lies on the surface. Hegel's constant use of the words Reason, Spirit, and the alleged supremacy he accorded Logic (in his peculiar understanding of logic) have deceived the would-be elect. To get below the surface, we have to lay hold of the force of the distinction he drew between reason or *Vernunft* and *Verstand* or understanding. Reflection, inquiry, observation and experimentation to test ideas and theories, all that we of the lesser breeds call intelligence, belongs in the Hegelian scheme to mere "understanding," which reason scorns and leaves behind in its sublime flight.

Especial point is given to the sharp separation of reflective intelligence and what is called reason in the teachings of Hegel's philosophy of history. "Understanding is the mode of mind which seeks precision and insists upon distinctions which are fixed." Accordingly it is at home in science (*mere* science as the Hegelian would say) and in all matters of calculation. Modern economic life is marked precisely by the manifestation of "understanding"; calculation and measurement are its determining factors. The bourgeois phase of society is accordingly identified by Hegel with operation of the understanding. According to him it has a necessary but strictly subordinate place in the structure of organized society. Beneath and above it is the creative work of reason which penetrates below distinctions to identities and rises above differences to unity.

History is the manifestation of this creative reason. In formation of historic peoples and in creation of their characteristic institutions, reason operates unconsciously.

Human beings act according to their impulses, passions, desires and private egotisms. They suppose they are doing their own work and fulfilling their own destiny. Actually, they are organs, agents of the divine absolute spirit, and are realizing its purposes. Only after absolute rational will has done its work may reflection supervene, and see what has been accomplished, in its true, its philosophic, meaning. But intelligence cannot create; it can only register what absolute reason has created, in its poor use of passion, desire, and "finite" human purpose. Reflective intelligence is like the "owl of Minerva which takes its flight only when the shades of evening have fallen"—when, that is, creative reason has completed one historic phase of its unconscious creative work.

The fact that Reason, working according to the process to which Hegel gives the name "logic," operates blindly and unconsciously as far as the agents of its execution are concerned, provides a genuine bond between it, in spite of the high eulogistic phraseology of Hegel, and the reliance of Hitler upon instinct. The bond of continuity is reinforced when we learn that the supreme *historic* manifestation of Absolute Spirit is its creation of nations; and that, in the history of the world, "a particular nation is dominant in a given epoch, so that in comparison with its absolute right as the bearer of the current phase of development of absolute spirit, the spirits of other nations are void of authority and no longer count in history." No great difficulty stood in the way of translating Hegel's state, which he often calls "nation," into

Hitler's Folk-community, and Hitler often expressly identifies nature, life, blood, with reason.

The chief bond of connection, however, is that after all Hegel's reason operates practically exclusively in the medium of the impulse, passion, desire, ambition, of personal or "subjective" wills, who unconsciously execute the will of absolute spirit, or Hegel's "God." It is perhaps worth noting that on one occasion Hegel, after mentioning the "cloudy undeveloped spirit of the Germans," went on to say, "If they are once forced to cast off their inaction, if they rouse themselves to action and realize the intensity of their inner life in contact with outward things, they will perhaps surpass their teachers" —the latter being, as the context shows, the French of the Revolutionary and the Napoleonic periods. Hitler might well claim to be the executor of the mission anticipated by Hegel. The one marked change is substitution of the "*volkische* society" for the political state— and even here Hegel's use of the word "nation" is loose enough to permit the transition.

In the course of the foregoing discussion, it was incidentally noted that Hitler holds the principle of democracy to be that of rule by a majority, and hence the subjection of "personality to mere numbers." He joins to this view of democracy on its political side, the view that, in its social phase, democracy is committed to an economic individualism which pulverizes all opportunity for social unity, and thereby weakens democratic countries so as to render them the easy prey of unified and "socialized" Germany. The democratic spirit of the United States has generally failed to make known abroad its working philosophy as a way of life. For while propaganda aims enter into what Hitler has said about democracy, what is just cited presents upon the whole his actual belief about democracy.

Hitler's failure to appreciate the philosophy of the democratic method of evolving social unity is the counterpart of his reliance upon authoritarian absolutistic force as the sole method of attaining social unity. Events have proved that there is something in German culture and education (Hitler calls it blood) which prevents Germans from appreciating and from trying the democratic method of attaining social unity, and which thereby evokes its response to appeal to achieve unity by the contrary method of force. An acute observer after years of association with Germans remarked to me that in no intellectual matter does the great mass of Germans have any use for discussion and conversation. They depend upon *ipse dixits*, upon finality of utterance, upon telling and being told. And this report of experience reminds me of what an engineer of European education told me: namely, that it required ten years of association with American engineers responsible for the conduct of a large productive industry to enable him to realize the force of the American method of back-and-forth give-and-take discussion until final decision represented a workable consensus of the ideas of all who took part.

Until he reached that stage of development, he had felt it necessary, he said, to try to drive home *his* point.

I conclude, then, with expression of the belief that it is this method, the method of achieving community by processes of free and open communication, which is the heart and the strength of the American democratic way of living and that the weaknesses of our democracy all represent expressions of failure to live up to the demands imposed by this method. Prejudices of economic status, of race, of religion, imperil democracy because they set up barriers to communication, or deflect and distort its operation. This is not the place to go into the relation of socialization of industrial production and distribution to attainment of a genuinely democratic way of life. But we can at least be sure that so far as the methods of management of a shop, a factory, a railway, or a bank are autocratic and hence harmful to democracy, it is because these methods prevent or impede the processes of effective give-and-take communication, of conference, of consultation, of exchange and pooling of experiences—of free conversation if you will.

Compartmentalizing of "science" is a distinctive feature of German life. It is this compartmentalization which enables Hitler, along with the high technical scientific development of Germany, to reduce all forms of science, physical, psychological, and social, to sheer tools of Nazi policy. The lesson for democracy is that science places in our hands an immensely valuable resource for rendering the processes of communication genuinely intelligent, so as to take them out of the field

of mere opinion as well as out of that of finality and
ipse dixit "authority." While reduction of scientific
method and scientific conclusions to a compartment that
is external to social life is distinctively German, it is not
confined to Germany. We have inherited that tendency;
the heritage shows itself, with harm to democracy, whenever and wherever we fail to use science as a means of
rendering communication more intelligent in all matters
requiring social decision.

As yet we have no adequately developed American
philosophy, because we have not as yet made articulate
the methods and aims of the democratic way of life. Out
and out use of force as the means of realizing the ideal
of social unity should then, at the very least, remind
us of the meaning of the alternative democratic method
for the continuous developing of social unity. The philosophy which formulates that method will be one which
acknowledges the primacy of communication in alliance
with those processes of patient extensive observation
and constant experimental test which are the human
and social significance of science.

The concluding pages of the chapters written over
twenty-five years ago stated with emphasis that the situation which then existed "presents the spectacle of the
breakdown of the whole philosophy of Nationalism, political, racial and cultural." They also suggested that our
own country is not free from the guilt of swollen nationalism. Without reviving here the question of "isolation-
ism" versus "interventionism" which events have
decided, it is fitting to note that the isolationist plea

for "America First," and the reasons it put forth in behalf of that plea, was animated by an uncurbed nationalist spirit of the sort which has brought the world to its present tragic state. The ever-increasing interdependence of peoples in every phase of modern life does not automatically bring understanding, amity and cooperation of the interdependent elements. As the state of the world proves, it may produce tensions and frictions, and these may lead each element to try at once to withdraw into itself and to establish peace and unity by forceful conquest of opposing elements.

The democratic principle of communication as the means of establishing unity applies to relations between nations as well as domestically. I do not think it is inappropriate to repeat the warning uttered many years ago about the danger of depending, when the war ends with victory over Fascist nations, exclusively upon judicial and political policies and agencies. They are necessary. But in the coming peace, as in the so-called peace of 1918, they will be effective only in connection with means and methods which make the inescapable facts of interdependence a positive and constructive reality in the lives of all of us, in "promoting the efficacy of human intercourse irrespective of class, racial, geographical and national limits." We shall play our own proper part in this work in the degree in which we make free communication a reality in all the phases and aspects of our own social life, domestic and trans-national.

I have tried in the foregoing pages to give an analysis of the theory and practice of Hitlerian Naziism in its own terms. Such an analysis has to be conducted in cool, dispassionate terms. But its outcome can and should produce an emotional response nonetheless intense because it is based upon understanding the nature of the enemy we have to meet. War with a totalitarian power is war against an aggressive way of life that can maintain itself in existence only by constant extension of its sphere of aggression. It is war against the invasion of organized force into every aspect and phase of life;—an invasion which regards its success within Germany as the sure promise of greater success throughout the whole world. And by use of the same methods of organizing every aspect of science and every form of technology to impose a servile straitjacket of conformity, to which the high title of social unity is given. We are committed by the challenge addressed to every element of a democratic way of life to use knowledge, technology, and every form of human relationship in order to promote social unity by means of free companionship and free communication. It is immensely clearer than it has ever been before that the democratic way of life commits us to unceasing effort to break down the walls of class, of unequal opportunity, of color, race, sect, and nationality, which estranges human beings from one another.

I

GERMAN PHILOSOPHY:

THE TWO WORLDS

The nature of the influence of general ideas upon practical affairs is a troubled question. Mind dislikes to find itself a pilgrim in an alien world. A discovery that the belief in the influence of thought upon action is an illusion would leave men profoundly saddened with themselves and with the world. Were it not that the doctrine forbids any discovery influencing affairs—since the discovery would be an idea—we should say that the discovery of the wholly *ex post facto* and idle character of ideas would profoundly influence subsequent affairs. The strange thing is that when men had least control over nature and their own affairs, they were most sure of the efficacy of thought. The doctrine that nature does nothing in vain, that it is directed by purpose, was not engrafted by scholasticism upon science; it formulates an instinctive tendency. And if the doctrine be fallacious,

51

its pathos has a noble quality. It testifies to the longing
of human thought for a world of its own texture. Yet just
in the degree in which men, by means of inventions
and political arrangements, have found ways of making
their thoughts effective, they have come to question
whether any thinking is efficacious. Our notions in physical science tend to reduce mind to a bare spectator of
a machine-like nature grinding its unrelenting way. The
vogue of evolutionary ideas has led many to regard intelligence as a deposit from history, not as a force in
its making. We look backward rather than forward; and
when we look forward we seem to see but a further
unrolling of a panorama long ago rolled up on a cosmic
reel. Even Bergson, who, to a casual reader, appears
to reveal vast unexplored vistas of genuinely novel possibilities, turns out, upon careful study, to regard *intellect*
(everything which in the past has gone by the name of
observation and reflection) as but an evolutionary deposit whose importance is confined to the conservation
of a life already achieved, and bids us trust to instinct,
or something akin to instinct, for the future:—as if there
were hope and consolation in bidding us trust to that
which, in any case, we cannot intelligently direct or
control.

I do not see that the school of history which finds
Bergson mystic and romantic, which prides itself upon
its hard-headed and scientific character, comes out at a
different place. I refer to the doctrine of the economic
interpretation of history in its extreme form—which, so
its adherents tell us, is its only logical form. It is easy

to follow them when they tell us that past historians have ignored the great part played by economic forces, and that descriptions and explanations have been correspondingly superficial. When one reflects that the great problems of the present day are those attending economic reorganization, one might even take the doctrine as a half-hearted confession that historians are really engaged in construing the past in terms of the problems and interests of an impending future, instead of reporting a past in order to discover some mathematical curve which future events are bound to describe. But no; our strictly scientific economic interpreters will have it that economic forces present an inevitable evolution, of which state and church, art and literature, science and philosophy are by-products. It is useless to suggest that while modern industry has given an immense stimulus to scientific inquiry, yet nevertheless the industrial revolution of the eighteenth century comes after the scientific revolution of the seventeenth. The dogma forbids any connection.

But when we note that Marx gave it away that his materialistic interpretation of history was but the Hegelian idealistic dialectic turned upside down, we may grow wary. Is it, after all, history with which we are dealing or another philosophy of history? And when we discover that the great importance of the doctrine is urged upon us, when we find that we are told that the general recognition of its truth helps us out of our present troubles and indicates a path for future effort, we positively take heart. These writers do not seem to mean just what they say. Like the rest of us, they are human, and infected with a belief that ideas, even highly abstract theories, are of efficacy in the conduct of human affairs influencing the history which is yet to be.

I have, however, no intention of entering upon this controversy, much less of trying to settle it. These remarks are but preliminary to a consideration of some of the practical affiliations of portions of the modern history of philosophical thought with practical social affairs. And if I set forth my own position in the controversy in question, the statement is frankly a personal one, intended to make known the prepossessions with which I approach the discussion of the political bearings of one phase of modern philosophy. I do not believe, then, that *pure* ideas, or pure thought, ever exercised any influence upon human action. I believe that very much of what has been presented as philosophic reflection is in effect simply an idealization, for the sake of emotional satisfaction, of the brutely given state of affairs, and is not a genuine discovery of the practical influence of ideas. In other words, I believe it to be æsthetic in type even when sadly lacking in æsthetic form. And I believe it is easy to exaggerate the practical influence of even the more vital and genuine ideas of which I am about to speak.

But I also believe that there are no such things as *pure* ideas or *pure* reason. Every living thought represents a gesture made toward the world, an attitude taken to some practical situation in which we are implicated. Most of these gestures are ephemeral; they reveal the state of him who makes them rather than effect a significant alteration of conditions. But at some times they are congenial to a situation in which men in masses are acting and suffering. They supply a model for the attitudes of others; they condense into a dramatic type of action. They then form what we call the "great" systems of thought. Not all ideas perish with the momentary response. They are voiced and others hear; they are written and others read. Education, formal and informal, embodies them not so much in other men's minds as in their permanent dispositions of action. They are in the blood, and afford sustenance to conduct; they are in the muscles and men strike or retire. Even emotional and æsthetic systems may breed a disposition toward the world and take overt effect. The reactions thus engendered are, indeed, superficial as compared with those in which more primitive instincts are embodied. The business of eating and drinking, buying and selling, marrying and being given in marriage, making war and peace, gets somehow carried on along with any and every system of ideas which the world has known. But how, and when and where and for what men do even these things is tremendously affected by the abstract ideas which get into circulation.

I take it that I may seem to be engaged in an emphatic urging of the obvious. However it may be with a few specialized schools of men, almost everybody takes it as a matter of course that ideas influence action and help determine the subsequent course of events. Yet there is a purpose in this insistence. Most persons draw the line at a certain kind of general ideas. They are especially prone to regard the ideas which constitute philosophic theories as practically innocuous—as more or less amiable speculations significant at the most for moments of leisure, in moments of relief from preoccupation with affairs. Above all, men take the particular general ideas which happen to affect their own conduct of life as normal and inevitable. Pray what other ideas would any sensible man have? They forget the extent to which these ideas originated as parts of a remote and technical theoretical system, which by multitudes of nonreflective channels has infiltrated into their habits of imagination and behavior. An expert intellectual anatomist, my friends, might dissect you and find Platonic and Aristotelian tissues, organs from St. Augustine and St. Thomas Aquinas, Locke and Descartes, in the make-up of the ideas by which you are habitually swayed, and find, indeed, that they and other thinkers of whose names you have never heard constitute a larger part of your mental structure than does the Calvin or Kant, Darwin or Spencer, Hegel or Emerson, Bergson or Browning to whom you yield conscious allegiance.

Philosophers themselves are naturally chiefly responsible for the ordinary estimate of their own influence, or lack of influence. They have been taken mostly at their own word as to what they were doing, and what for the most part they have pretended to do is radically different from what they have actually done. They are quite negligible as seers and reporters of ultimate reality and the essential natures of things. And it is in this aspect that they have mostly fancied seeing themselves. Their actual office has been quite other. They have told about nature and life and society in terms of collective human desire and aspiration as these were determined by contemporary difficulties and struggles.

I have spoken thus far as if the influence of general ideas upon action were likely to be beneficial. It goes against the grain to attribute evil to the workings of intelligence. But we might as well face the dilemma. What is called pure thought, thought freed from the empirical contingencies of life, would, even if it existed, be irrelevant to the guidance of action. For the latter always operates amid the circumstance of contingencies. And thinking which is colored by time and place must always be of a mixed quality. In part, it will detect and hold fast to more permanent tendencies and arrangements; in part, it will take the limitations of its own period as necessary and universal—even as intrinsically desirable.

The traits which give thinking effectiveness for the good give it also potency for harm. A physical catastrophe, an earthquake or conflagration, acts only where it happens. While its effects endure, it passes away. But it is of the nature of ideas to be abstract: that is to say, severed from the circumstances of their origin, and through embodiment in language capable of operating in remote climes and alien situations. Time heals physical ravages, but it may only accentuate the evils of an intellectual catastrophe—for by no lesser name can we call a systematic intellectual error. To one who is professionally preoccupied with philosophy there is much in its history whiich is profoundly depressing. He sees ideas which were not only natural but useful in their native time and place, figuring in foreign contexts so as to formulate defects as virtues and to give rational sanction to brute facts, and to oppose alleged eternal truths to progress. He sees movements which might have passed away with change of circumstance as casually as they arose, acquire persistence and dignity because thought has taken cognizance of them and given them intellectual names. The witness of history is that to think in general and abstract terms is dangerous; it elevates ideas beyond the situations in which they were born and charges them with we know not what menace for the future. And in the past the danger has been the greater because philosophers have so largely purported to be concerned not with contemporary problems of living, but with essential Truth and Reality viewed under the form of eternity.

In bringing these general considerations to a close, I face an embarrassment. I must choose some particular period of intellectual history for more concrete illustration of the mutual relationship of philosophy and practical social affairs—which latter, for the sake of brevity, I term Politics. One is tempted to choose Plato. For in spite of the mystic and transcendental coloring of his thought, it was he who defined philosophy as the science of the State, or the most complete and organized whole known to man; it is no accident that his chief work is termed the "Republic." In modern times, we are struck by the fact that English philosophy from Bacon to John Stuart Mill has been cultivated by men of affairs rather than by professors, and with a direct outlook upon social interests. In France, the great period of philosophy, the period of *les philosophes*, was the time in which were forged the ideas which connect in particular with the French Revolution and in general with the conceptions which spread so rapidly through the civilized world, of the indefinite perfectibility of humanity, the rights of man, and the promotion of a society as wide as humanity, based upon allegiance to reason.

Somewhat arbitrarily I have, however, selected some aspects of classic German thought for my illustrative material. Partly, I suppose, because one is piqued by the apparent challenge which its highly technical, professorial and predominantly *a priori* character offers to the proposition that there is close connection between abstract thought and the tendencies of collective life. More to the point, probably, is the fact that the heroic age of German thought lies almost within the last century, while the creative period of continental thought lies largely in the eighteenth century, and that of British thought still earlier. It was Taine, the Frenchman, who said that all the leading ideas of the present day were produced in Germany between 1780 and 1830. Above all, the Germans, as we say, have philosophy in their blood. Such phrases generally mean something not about hereditary qualities, but about the social conditions under which ideas propagate and circulate.

Now Germany is the modern state which provides the

greatest facilities for general ideas to take effect through social inculcation. Its system of education is adapted to that end. Higher schools and universities in Germany are really, not just nominally, under the control of the state and part of the state life. In spite of freedom of academic instruction when once a teacher is installed in office, the political authorities have always taken a hand, at critical junctures, in determining the selection of teachers in subjects that had a direct bearing upon political policies. Moreover, one of the chief functions of the universities is the preparation of future state officials. Legislative activity is distinctly subordinate to that of administration conducted by a trained civil service, or, if you please, bureaucracy. Membership in this bureaucracy is dependent upon university training. Philosophy, both directly and indirectly, plays an unusually large role in the training. The faculty of law does not chiefly aim at the preparation of practicing lawyers. Philosophies of jurisprudence are essential parts of the law teaching; and every one of the classic philosophers took a hand in writing a philosophy of Law and of the State. Moreover, in the theological faculties, which are also organic parts of state-controlled institutions, the theology and higher criticism of Protestant Germany have been developed, and developed also in close connection with philosophical systems—like those of Kant, Schleiermacher and Hegel. In short, the educational and administrative agencies of Germany provide ready-made channels through which philosophic ideas may flow on their way to practical affairs.

Political public opinion hardly exists in Germany in the sense in which it obtains in France, Great Britain or this country. So far as it exists, the universities may be said to be its chief organs. They, rather than the newspapers, crystallize it and give it articulate expression. Instead of expressing surprise at the characteristic utterances of university men with reference to the great war, we should then rather turn to the past history in which the ideas now uttered were generated.

In an account of German intellectual history sufficiently extensive we should have to go back at least to Luther. Fortunately, for our purposes, what he actually did and taught is not so important as the more recent tradition concerning his peculiarly Germanic status and office. All peoples are proud of all their great men. Germany is proud of Luther as its greatest national hero. But while most nations are proud of their great men, Germany is proud of itself rather for producing Luther. It finds him as a Germanic product quite natural—nay, inevitable. A belief in the universal character of his genius thus naturally is converted into a belief of the essentially universal quality of the people who produced him.

Heine was not disposed by birth or temperament to overestimate the significance of Luther. But here is what he said:

"Luther is not only the greatest but the most *German* man in our history.... He possessed qualities that we seldom see associated—nay, that we usually find in the most hostile antagonism. He was at once a dreamy mystic and a practical man of action.... He was both a cold scholastic word-sifter and an inspired God-drunk prophet.... He was full of the awful reverence of God, full of self-sacrificing devotion to the Holy Spirit, he could lose himself entirely in pure spirituality. Yet he was fully acquainted with the glories of this earth; he knew how estimable they are; it was his lips that uttered the famous maxim—

> " 'Who loves not woman, wine and song,
>   Remains a fool his whole life long.'

He was a complete man, I might say an absolute man, in whom there was no discord between matter and spirit. To call him a spiritualist would be as erroneous as to call him a sensualist.... Eternal praise to the man whom we have to thank for the deliverance of our most precious possessions."

And again speaking of Luther's work:

"Thus was established in Germany spiritual freedom, or as it is called, freedom of thought. Thought became a right and the decisions of reason legitimate."

The specific correctness of the above is of slight importance as compared with the universality of the tradition which made these ideas peculiarly Germanic, and Luther, therefore, a genuine national hero and type.

It is, however, with Kant that I commence. In Protestant Germany his name is almost always associated with that of Luther. That he brought to consciousness the true meaning of the Lutheran reformation is a commonplace of the German historian. One can hardly convey a sense of the unique position he occupies in the German thought of the last two generations. It is not that every philosopher is a Kantian, or that the professed Kantians stick

literally to his text. Far from it. But Kant must always
be reckoned with. No position unlike his should be taken
up till Kant has been reverently disposed of, and the new
position evaluated in his terms. To scoff at him is fair
sacrilege. In a genuine sense, he marks the end of the
older age. He *is* the transition to distinctively modern
thought.

One shrinks at the attempt to compress even his leading ideas into an hour. Fortunately for me, few who
read my attempt will have sufficient acquaintance with
the tomes of Kantian interpretation and exposition to
appreciate the full enormity of my offense. For I cannot
avoid the effort to seize from out his highly technical
writings a single idea and to label that his germinal idea.
For only in this way can we get a clew to those general
ideas with which Germany characteristically prefers to
connect the aspirations and convictions that animate its
deeds.

Adventuring without further preface into this field, I
find that Kant's decisive contribution is the idea of a
dual legislation of reason which marks off two distinct
realms—one of science, the other that of morals. Each
of these two realms has its own final and authoritative
constitution: On one hand, there is the world of sense,
the world of phenomena in space and time in which
science is at home; on the other hand, is the supersensible, the noumenal world, the world of moral duty and
moral freedom.

Every cultivated man is familiar with the conflict of
science and religion, brute fact and ideal purpose, what

is and what ought to be, necessity and freedom. In the domain of science causal dependence is sovereign; while freedom is lord of moral action. It is the proud boast of those who are Kantian in spirit that Kant discovered laws deep in the very nature of things and of human experience whose recognition puts an end forever to all possibility of conflict.

In principle, the discovery is as simple as its application is far-reaching. Both science and moral obligation exist. Analysis shows that each is based upon laws supplied by one and the same reason (of which, as he is fond of saying, reason is the legislator); but laws of such a nature that their respective jurisdictions can never compete. The material for the legislation of reason in the natural world is sense. In this sensible world of space and time, causal necessity reigns: such is the decree of reason itself. Every attempt to find freedom, to locate ideals, to draw support for man's moral aspirations in nature, is predoomed to failure. The effort of reason to do these things is contrary to the very nature of reason itself: it is self-contradictory, suicidal.

When one considers the extent in which religion has been bound up with belief in miracles, or departures from the order of nature; when one notes how support for morals has been sought in natural law; how morals have been tied up with man's natural tendencies to seek happiness and with consequences in the way of reward of virtue and punishment of vice; how history has been explained as a play of moral forces—in short, the extent to which both the grounds and the sanctions for morality have been sought within the time and space world, one realizes the scope of the revolution wrought by Kant, provided his philosophy be true. Add to this the fact that men in the past have not taken seriously the idea that every existence in space, every event in time, is connected by bonds of causal necessity with other existences and events, and consequently have had no motive for the systematic pursuit of science. How is the late appearance of science in human history to be accounted for? How are we to understand the comparatively slight influence which science still has upon the conduct of life? Men, when they have not consciously looked upon nature as a scene of caprice, have failed to bring home to themselves that nature is a scene of the legislative activity of reason in the material of sense. This fact the Kantian philosophy brings home to man once for all; it brings it home not as a pious wish, nor as a precarious hope confirmed empirically here and there by victories won by a Galileo or a Newton, but as an indubitable fact necessary to the existence of any cognitive experience at all. The reign of law in nature is the work of the same reason which proceeds empirically and haltingly to the discovery of law here and there. Thus the acceptance of the Kantian philosophy seemed to his followers not only to free man at a single stroke from superstition, sentimentalism and moral and theological romanticism, but to give at the same stroke authorization and stimulation to the detailed efforts of man to wrest from nature her secrets of causal law. What sparse groups of men of natural science had been doing for the three preceding centuries, Kant proclaimed to be the manifestation of the essential constitution of man as a knowing being. For those who accept the Kantian philosophy, it is accordingly the *magna charta* of scientific work: the adequate formulation of the constitution which directs and justifies their scientific inquiries. It is a truism to say that among the Germans as nowhere else has developed a positive reverence for science. In what other land does one find in the organic law mention of Science, and read in its constitution an express provision that "Science and its teaching are free"?

But this expresses only half of Kant's work. Reason is itself supersensible. Giving law to the material of sense and so constituting nature, it is in itself above sense and nature, as a sovereign is above his subjects. The supersensible world is thus a more congenial field for its legislative activity than the physical world of space and time. But is any such field open to human experience? Has not Kant himself closed and locked the gates in his assertion that the entire operation of man's knowing powers is confined to the realm of sense in which causal necessity dominates? Yes, as far as knowledge is concerned. No, as far as moral obligation is concerned. The fact of duty, the existence of a categorical command to act thus and so, no matter what the pressure of physical surroundings or the incitation of animal inclinations, is as much a fact as the existence of knowledge of the physical world. Such a command cannot proceed from nature. What is cannot introduce man to what ought to be, and thus impose its own opposite upon him. Nature

only enmeshes men in its relentless machine-like movement. The very existence of a command in man to act
for the sake of what ought to be—no matter what actually
is—is thus of itself final proof of the operation of supersensible reason within human experience: not, indeed,
within theoretical or cognitive experience, but within
moral experience.

The moral law, the law of obligation, thus proceeds
from a source in man above reason. It is token of his
membership as a moral being in a kingdom of absolute ends above nature. But it is also directed to something in man which is equally above nature: it appeals to
and demands freedom. Reason is incapable of anything
so irrational, so self-contradictory, as imposing a law
of action to which no faculty of action corresponds.
The freedom of the moral will is the answer to the
unqualified demand of duty. It is not open to man to
accept or reject this truth as he may see fit. It is a principle of reason which is involved in every exercise of
reason. In denying it in name, man none the less acknowledges it in fact. Only men already sophisticated by
vice who are seeking an excuse for their viciousness ever
try to deny, even in words, the response which freedom
makes to the voice of duty. Since, however, freedom is
an absolute stranger to the natural and sensible world,
man's possession of moral freedom is the final sign and
seal of his membership in a supersensible world. The
existence of an ideal or spiritual realm with its own laws
is thus certified to by the fact of man's own citizenship
within it. But, once more, this citizenship and this certifi-

cation are solely moral. Scientific or intellectual warrant for it is impossible or self-contradictory, for science works by the law of causal necessity with respect to what is, ignorant of any law of freedom referring to what should be.

With the doors to the supersensible world now open, it is but a short step to religion. Of the negative traits of true religion we may be sure in advance. It will not be based upon intellectual grounds. Proofs of the existence of God, of the creation of nature, of the existence of an immaterial soul from the standpoint of knowledge are all of them impossible. They transgress the limits of knowledge, since that is confined to the sensible world of time and space. Neither will true religion be based upon historic facts such as those of Jewish history or the life of Jesus or the authority of a historic institution like a church. For all historic facts as such fall within the realm of time which is sensibly conditioned. From the points of view of natural theology and historic religions Kant was greeted by his contemporaries as the "all-shattering." Quite otherwise is it, however, as to moral proofs of religious ideas and ideals. In Kant's own words: "I have found it necessary to deny knowledge of God, freedom and immortality in order to find a place for faith" —faith being a moral act.

Then he proceeds to reinterpret in terms of the sensuous natural principle and the ideal rational principle the main doctrines of Lutheran Protestantism. The doctrines of incarnation, original sin, atonement, justification by faith and sanctification, while baseless literally and his-

torically, are symbols of the dual nature of man, as phenomenal and noumenal. And while Kant scourges
ecclesiastical religions so far as they have relied upon
ceremonies and external authority, upon external rewards
and punishments, yet he ascribes transitional value to
them in that they have symbolized ultimate moral truths.
Although dogmas are but the external vesture of inner
truths, yet it may be good for us "to continue to pay
reverence to the outward vesture since that has served to
bring to general acceptance a doctrine which really rests
upon an authority within the soul of man, and which,
therefore, needs no miracle to commend it."

It is a precarious undertaking to single out some one
thing in German philosophy as of typical importance in
understanding German national life. Yet I am committed
to the venture. My conviction is that we have its root idea
in the doctrine of Kant concerning the two realms, one
outer, physical and necessary, the other inner, ideal and
free. To this we must add that, in spite of their separate-
ness and independence, the primacy always lies with the
inner. As compared with this, the philosophy of a
Nietzsche, to which so many resort at the present time for
explanation of what seems to them otherwise inex-
plicable, is but a superficial and transitory wave of
opinion. Surely the chief mark of distinctively German
civilization is its combination of self-conscious idealism
with unsurpassed technical efficiency and organization in
the varied fields of action. If this is not a realization in
fact of what is found in Kant, I am totally at loss for a
name by which to characterize it. I do not mean that con-

scious adherence to the philosophy of Kant has been the cause of the marvelous advances made in Germany in the natural sciences and in the systematic application of the fruits of intelligence to industry, trade, commerce, military affairs, education, civic administration and industrial organization. Such a claim would be absurd. But I do mean, primarily, that Kant detected and formulated the direction in which the German genius was moving, so that his philosophy is of immense prophetic significance; and, secondarily, that his formulation has furnished a banner and a conscious creed which in solid and definite fashion has intensified and deepened the work actually undertaken.

In bringing to an imaginative synthesis what might have remained an immense diversity of enterprises, Kantianism has helped formulate a sense of a national mission and destiny. Over and above this, his formulation and its influence aids us to understand why the German consciousness has never been swamped by its technical efficiency and devotion, but has remained self-consciously, not to say self-righteously, idealistic. Such a work as Germany has undertaken might well seem calculated to generate attachment to a positivistic or even materialistic philosophy and to a utilitarian ethics. But no; the teaching of Kant had put mechanism forever in its subordinate place at the very time it inculcated devotion to mechanism in its place. Above and beyond as an end, for the sake of which all technical achievements, all promotion of health, wealth and happiness, exist, lies the realm of inner freedom, of the ideal and the supersensible. The more the Germans accomplish in the way of material conquest, the more they are conscious of fulfilling an ideal mission; every external conquest affords the greater warrant for dwelling in an inner region where mechanism does not intrude. Thus it turns out that while the Germans have been, to employ a catchword of recent thought, the most rigidly and narrowly pragmatic of all peoples in their actual conduct of affairs, there is no people so hostile to the spirit of a pragmatic philosophy.

The combination of devotion to mechanism and organization in outward affairs and of loyalty to freedom and consciousness in the inner realm has its obvious attractions. Realized in the common temper of a people it might well seem invincible. Ended is the paralysis of action arising from the split between science and useful achievements on one side and spiritual and ideal aspirations on the other. Each feeds and reinforces the other. Freedom of soul and subordination of action dwell in harmony. Obedience, definite subjection and control, detailed organization is the lesson enforced by the rule of causal necessity in the outer world of space and time in which action takes place. Unlimited freedom, the heightening of consciousness for its own sake, sheer reveling in noble ideals, the law of the inner world. What more can mortal man ask?

It would not be difficult, I imagine, to fill the three hours devoted to these lectures with quotations from representative German authors to the effect that supreme regard for the inner meaning of things, reverence for inner truth in disregard of external consequences of advantage or disadvantage, is the distinguishing mark of the German spirit as against, say, the externality of the Latin spirit or the utilitarianism of Anglo-Saxondom. I content myself with one quotation, a quotation which also indicates the same inclination to treat historic facts as symbolic of great truths which is found in Kant's treatment of church dogmas. Speaking of the Germanic languages, an historian of German civilization says:

"While all other Indo-European languages allow a wide liberty in placing the accent and make external considerations, such as the quantity of the syllables and euphony, of deciding influence, the Germanic tribes show a remarkable and intentional transition to an internal principle of accentuation.... Of all related peoples the Germanic alone puts the accent on the root syllable of the word, that is, on the part that gives it its meaning. There is hardly an ethnological fact extant which gives so much food for thought as this. What leads these people to give up a habit which must have been so old that it had become instinctive, and to evolve out of their own minds a principle which indicates a power of discrimination far in advance of anything we are used to attribute to the lower stages of civilization? Circumstances of which we are not now aware must have compelled them to distinguish the inner essence of things from their external form, and must have taught them to appreciate the former as of higher, indeed as of sole, importance. It is this accentuation of the real substance of things, the ever-powerful desire to discover this real substance, and the ever-present impulse to give expression to this inner reality which has become the controlling trait of the Germanic soul. Hence the conviction gained by countless unfruitful efforts, that reason alone will never get at the true foundation of things; hence the thoroughness of German science; hence a great many of the qualities that explain Germanic successes and failures; hence, perhaps, a certain stubbornness and obstinacy, the unwillingness to give up a conviction once formed; hence the tendency to mysticism; hence that continuous struggle which marks the history of German art,—the struggle to give to the contents powerful and adequate expression, and to satisfy at the same time the requirements of æsthetic elegance and beauty, a struggle in which the victory is ever on the side of truth, though it be homely, over beauty of form whenever it appears deceitful; hence the part played by music as the only expression of those imponderable vibrations of the soul for which language seems to have no words; hence the faith of the German in his mission among the nations as a bringer of truth, as a recognizer of the real value of things as against the hollow shell of beautiful form, as the doer of right deeds for their own sake and not for any reward beyond the natural outcome of the deed itself."

The division established between the outer realm, in which of course acts fall, and the inner realm of consciousness explains what is otherwise so paradoxical to a foreigner in German writings: The constant assertion that Germany brought to the world the conscious recognition of the principle of freedom coupled with the assertion of the relative incompetency of the German folk *en masse* for political self-direction. To one saturated by the English tradition which identifies freedom with power to act upon one's ideas, to make one's purposes effective in regulation of public affairs, the combination seems self-contradictory. To the German it is natural. Readers who have been led by newspaper quotations to regard Bernhardi as preaching simply a gospel of superior force will find in his writings a continual assertion that *the* German spirit is the spirit of freedom, of complete intellectual self-determination; that the Germans have "always been the standard bearers of free thought." We find him supporting his teachings not by appeal to Nietzsche, but by the Kantian distinction between the "empirical and rational egos."

It is Bernhardi who says:

"Two great movements were born from the German intellectual life, on which, henceforth, *all the intellectual and moral progress of mankind must rest:*—The Reformation and the critical philosophy. The Reformation that broke the intellectual yoke imposed by the Church, which checked all free progress; and the Critique of Pure Reason which put a stop to the caprice of philosophic speculation by defining for the human mind the limitations of its capacities for knowledge, and at the same time pointed out the way in which knowledge is really possible. On this substructure was developed the intellectual life of our time, whose deepest significance consists in the attempt to reconcile the result of free inquiry with the religious needs of the heart, and thus to lay a foundation for the harmonious organization of mankind. . . . The German nation not only laid the foundations of this great struggle for a harmonious development of humanity but took the lead in it. We are thus incurring an obligation for the future from which we cannot shrink. We must be prepared to be the leader in this campaign which is being fought for the highest stake that has been offered to human efforts. . . . To no nation except the German has it been given to enjoy in its inner self 'that which is given to mankind as a whole.' . . . It is this quality which especially fits us for leadership in the intellectual domain and *imposes upon us the obligation to maintain that position.*" *

More significant than the words themselves are their occasion and the occupation of the one who utters them. Outside of Germany, cavalry generals who employ phi-

* Bernhardi, "Germany and the Next War," pp. 73-74. Italics not in the original text.

losophy to bring home practical lessons are, I think, rare. Outside of Germany, it would be hard to find an audience where an appeal for military preparedness would be reinforced by allusions to the Critique of Pure Reason.

Yet only by taking such statements seriously can one understand the temper in which opinion in Germany meets a national crisis. When the philosopher Eucken (who received a Nobel prize for contributing to the idealistic literature of the world) justifies the part taken by Germany in a world war because the Germans alone do not represent a particularistic and nationalistic spirit, but embody the "universalism" of humanity itself, he utters a conviction bred in German thought by the ruling interpretation of German philosophic idealism. By the side of this *motif* the glorification of war as a biologic necessity, forced by increase of population, is a secondary detail, giving a totally false impression when isolated from its context. The main thing is that Germany, more than any other nation, in a sense alone of all nations, embodies the essential principle of humanity: freedom of spirit, combined with thorough and detailed work in the outer sphere where reigns causal law, where obedience, discipline and subordination are the necessities of successful organization. It is perhaps worth while to recall that Kant lived, taught and died in Königsberg; and that Königsberg was the chief city of east Prussia, an island still cut off in his early years from western Prussia, a titular capital for the Prussian kings where they went for their coronations. His life-work in philos-

ophy coincides essentially with the political work of
Frederick the Great, the king who combined a régime of
freedom of thought and complete religious toleration
with the most extraordinary display known in history of
administrative and military efficiency. Fortunately for
our present purposes, Kant, in one of his minor essays,
has touched upon this combination and stated its philosophy in terms of his own thought.

The essay in question is that entitled "What is the
Enlightenment?" His reply in substance is that it is the
coming of age on the part of humanity: the transition
from a state of minority or infancy wherein man does not
dare to think freely to that period of majority or ma-
turity in which mankind dares to use its own power of
understanding. The growth of this power of free use of
reason is the sole hope of progress in human affairs.
External revolutions which are not the natural expression
of an inner or intellectual revolution are of little significance. Genuine growth is found in the slow growth of
science and philosophy and in the gradual diffusion
throughout the mass of the discoveries and conclusions
of those who are superior in intelligence. True freedom
is inner freedom, freedom of thought together with the
liberty consequent upon it of teaching and publication.
To check this rational freedom "is a sin against the very
nature of man, the primary law of which consists in just
the advance in rational enlightenment."

In contrast with this realm of inner freedom stands
that of civil and political action, the principle of which
is obedience or subordination to constituted authority.

Kant illustrates the nature of the two by the position of a military subordinate who is given an order to execute which his reason tells him is unwise. His sole duty in the realm of practice is to obey—to do his duty. But as a member not of the State but of the kingdom of science, he has the right of free inquiry and publication. Later he might write upon the campaign in which this event took place and point out, upon intellectual grounds, the mistake involved in the order. No wonder that Kant proclaims that the age of enlightenment is the age of Frederick the Great. Yet we should do injustice to Kant if we inferred that he expected this dualism of spheres of action, with its twofold moral law of freedom and obedience, to endure forever. By the exercise of freedom of thought, and by its publication and the education which should make its results permeate the whole state, the habits of a nation will finally become elevated to rationality, and the spread of reason will make it possible for the government to treat men, not as cogs in a machine, but in accord with the dignity of rational creatures.

Before leaving this theme, I must point out one aspect of the work of reason thus far passed over. Nature, the sensible world of space and time, is, as a knowable object, constituted by the legislative work of reason, although constituted out of a non-rational sensible stuff. This determining work of reason forms not merely the Idealism of the Kantian philosophy but determines its emphasis upon the *a priori*. The functions of reason through which nature is rendered a knowable object cannot be derived from experience, for they are necessary to the existence of experience. The details of this *a priori* apparatus lie far outside our present concern. Suffice it to say that as compared with some of his successors, Kant was an economical soul and got along with only two *a priori* forms and twelve *a priori* categories. The mental habitudes generated by attachment to *a priori* categories cannot however be entirely neglected in even such a cursory discussion as the present.

If one were to follow the suggestion involved in the lately quoted passage as to the significant symbolism of the place of the accent in German speech, one might discourse upon the deep meaning of the Capitalization of Nouns in the written form of the German language, together with the richness of the language in abstract nouns. One might fancy that the dignity of the common noun substantive, expressing as it does the universal or generic, has bred an intellectual deference. One may fancy a whole nation of readers reverently bowing their heads at each successively capitalized word. In such fashion one might arrive at a picture, not without its truth, of what it means to be devoted to *a priori* rational principles.

A number of times during the course of the world war I have heard someone remark that he would not so much mind what the Germans did if it were not for the reasons assigned in its justification. But to rationalize such a tangled skein as human experience is a difficult task. If one is in possession of antecedent rational concepts which are legislative for experience, the task is much simplified.

It only remains to subsume each empirical event under its proper category. If the outsider does not see the applicability of the concept to the event, it may be argued that his blindness shows his ineptness for truly universal thinking. He is probably a crass empiric who thinks in terms of material consequences instead of upon the basis of antecedent informing principles of reason.

Thus it has come about that no normal, social or political question is adequately discussed in Germany until the matter in hand has been properly deducted from an exhaustive determination of its fundamental *Begriff* or *Wesen*. Or if the material is too obviously empirical to allow of such deduction, it must at least be placed under its appropriate rational form. What a convenience, what resource, nay, what a weapon is the Kantian distinction of *a priori* rational form and *a posteriori* empirical matter. Let the latter be as brutely diversified, as chaotic as you please. There always exists a form of unity under which it may be brought. If the empirical facts are recalcitrant, so much the worse for them. It only shows how empirical they are. To put them under a rational form is but to subdue their irrational opposition to reason, or to invade their lukewarm neutrality. Any violence done them is more than indemnified by the favor of bringing them under the sway of *a priori* reason, the incarnation of the Absolute on earth.

Yet there are certain disadvantages attached to *a priori* categories. They have a certain rigidity, appalling to those who have not learned to identify stiffness with force. Empirical matters are subject to revision. The strongest belief that claims the support of experience is subject to modification when experience testifies against it. But an *a priori* conception is not open to adverse evidence. There is no court having jurisdiction. If, then, an unfortunate mortal should happen to be imposed upon so that he was led to regard a prejudice or predilection as an *a priori* truth, contrary experience would have a tendency to make him the more obstinate in his belief. History proves what a dangerous thing it has been for men, when they try to impose their will upon other men, to think of themselves as special instruments and organs of Deity. The danger is equally great when an *a priori* Reason is substituted for a Divine Providence. Empirically grounded truths do not have a wide scope; they do not inspire such violent loyalty to themselves as ideas supposed to proceed directly from reason itself. But they are discussable; they have a humane and social quality, while truths of pure reason have a paradoxical way, in the end, of escaping from the arbitrament of reasoning. They evade the logic of experience, only to become, in the phrase of a recent writer, the spoil of a "logic of fanaticism." Weapons forged in the smithy of the Absolute become brutal and cruel when confronted by merely human resistance.

The stiffly constrained character of an *a priori* Reason manifests itself in another way. A category of pure reason is suspiciously like a pigeon-hole. An American writer, speaking before the present war, remarked with witty exaggeration that "Germany is a monstrous set of pigeonholes, and every mother's son of a German is pigeoned in his respective hole—tagged, labeled and ticketed. Germany is a huge human check-room, and the government carries the checks in its pocket." John Locke's deepest objection to the older form of the *a priori* philosophy, the doctrine of innate ideas, was the readiness with which such ideas become strongholds behind which authority shelters itself from questioning. And John Morley pointed out long ago the undoubted historic fact that the whole modern liberal social and political movement has allied itself with philosophic empiricism. It is hard here, as everywhere, to disentangle cause and effect. But one can at least say with considerable assurance that a hierarchically ordered and subordered State will feel an affinity for a philosophy of fixed categories, while a flexible democratic society will, in its crude empiricism, exhibit loose ends.

There is a story to the effect that the good townspeople of Königsberg were accustomed to their watches by the time at which Kant passed upon his walks—so uniform was he. Yielding to the Teutonic temptation to find an inner meaning in the outer event, one may wonder whether German thought has not since Kant's time set its intellectual and spiritual clocks by the Kantian standard: the separation of the inner and the outer, with its lesson of freedom and idealism in one realm, and of mechanism, efficiency and organization in the other. A German professor of philosophy has said that while the Latins live in the present moment, the Germans live in the infinite and ineffable. His accusation (though I am not sure he meant it as such) is not completely justified. But it does seem to be true that the Germans, more readily than other peoples, can withdraw themselves from the exigencies and contingencies of life into a region of *Innerlichkeit* which at least *seems* boundless; and which can rarely be successfully uttered save through music, and a frail and tender poetry, sometimes domestic, sometimes lyric, but always full of mysterious charm. But technical ideas, ideas about means and instruments, can readily be externalized because the outer world is in truth their abiding home.

II

GERMAN MORAL

AND

POLITICAL PHILOSOPHY

It is difficult to select sentences from Kant which are intelligible to those not trained in his vocabulary, unless the selection is accompanied by an almost word-by-word commentary. His writings have proved an admirable *terrain* for the display of German *Gründlichkeit*. But I venture upon the quotation of one sentence which may serve the purpose of at once recalling the main lesson of the previous lecture and furnishing a transition to the theme of the present hour.

"Even if an immeasurable gulf is fixed between the sensible realm of the concept of nature and the supersensible realm of the concept of freedom, so that it is not possible to go from the first to the second (at least by means of the theoretical use of reason) any more than if they were two separate worlds of which the first could have no influence upon the second,— yet the second is *meant* to have an influence upon the first. The concept of freedom is meant to actualize in the world of sense the purpose proposed by its laws." ...

83

That is, the relation between the world of space and
time where physical causality reigns and the moral world
of freedom and duty is not a symmetrical one. The
former cannot intrude into the latter. But it is the very
nature of moral legislation that it is meant to influence
the world of sense; its object is to realize the purposes
of free rational action within the sense world. This fact
fixes the chief features of Kant's philosophy of Morals
and of the State.

It is a claim of the admirers of Kant that he first
brought to recognition the true and infinite nature of the
principle of Personality. On one side, the individual is
homo phenomenon—a part of the scheme of nature,
governed by its laws as much as any stone or plant. But
in virtue of his citizenship in the kingdom of supersensible Laws and Ends, he is elevated to true universality. He is no longer a mere occurrence. He is a Person—
one in whom the purpose of Humanity is incarnate. In
English and American writings the terms subjective and
subjectivism usually carry with them a disparaging color.
Quite otherwise is it in German literature. This sets the
age of subjectivism, whose commencement, roughly
speaking, coincides with the influence of Kantian thought,
in sharp opposition to the age of individualism, as well
as to a prior period of subordination to external authority. Individualism means isolation; it means external
relations of human beings with one another and with
the world; it looks at things quantitatively, in terms of
wholes and parts. Subjectivism means recognition of
the principle of free personality: the self as creative,

occupied not with an external world which limits it from without, but, through its own self-consciousness, finding a world within itself; and having found the universal within itself, setting to work to recreate itself in what had been the external world, and by its own creative expansion in industry, art and politics to transform what had been mere limiting material into a work of its own. Free as was Kant from the sentimental, the mystic and the romantic phases of this Subjectivism, we shall do well to bear it in mind in thinking of his ethical theory. Personality means that man as a rational being does not receive the end which forms the law of his action from without, whether from Nature, the State or from God, but from his own self. Morality is autonomous; man, humanity, is an end in itself. Obedience to the self-imposed law will transform the sensible world (within which falls all social ties so far as they spring from natural instinct desire) into a form appropriate to universal reason. Thus we may paraphrase the sentence quoted from Kant.

The gospel of duty has an invigorating ring. It is easy to present it as the most noble and sublime of all moral doctrines. What is more worthy of humanity, what better marks the separation of man from brute, than the will to subordinate selfish desire and individual inclination to the commands of stern and lofty duty? And if the idea of command (which inevitably goes with the notion of duty) carries a sinister suggestion of legal authority, pains and penalties and of subservience to an external authority who issues the commands, Kant seems to have provided a final corrective in insisting that duty is self-imposed. Moral commands are imposed by the higher, supranatural self upon the lower empirical self, by the rational self upon the self of passions and inclinations. German philosophy is attached to antitheses and their reconciliation in a higher synthesis. The Kantian principle of Duty is a striking case of the reconciliation of the seemingly conflicting ideas of freedom and authority.

Unfortunately, however, the balance cannot be maintained in practice. Kant's faithful logic compels him to insist that the concept of duty is empty and formal. It tells men that to do their duty is their supreme law of action, but is silent as to what men's duties specifically are. Kant, moreover, insists, as he is in logic bound to do, that the motive which measures duty is wholly inner; it is purely a matter of inner consciousness. To admit that consequences can be taken into account in deciding what duty is in a particular case would be to make concessions to the empirical and sensible world which are fatal to the scheme. The combination of these two features of pure internality and pure formalism leads, in a world where men's *acts* take place wholly in the external and empirical region, to serious consequences.

The dangerous character of these consequences may perhaps be best gathered indirectly by means of a quotation.

"While the French people in savage revolt against spiritual and secular despotism had broken their chains and proclaimed their *rights,* another quite different revolution was working in Prussia—the revolution of *duty.* The assertion of the rights of the individual leads ultimately to individual irresponsibility and to a repudiation of the State. Immanuel Kant, the founder of the critical philosophy, taught, in opposition to this view, the gospel of moral duty, and Scharnhorst grasped the idea of universal military service. By calling upon each individual to sacrifice property and life for the good of the community, he gave the clearest expression of the idea of the State, and created a sound basis on which the claims to individual rights might rest." *

The sudden jump, by means of only a comma, from the gospel of moral duty to universal military service is much more logical than the shock which it gives to an American reader would indicate. I do not mean, of course, that Kant's teaching was the cause of Prussia's adoption of universal military service and of the thor-ough-going subordination of individual happiness and liberty of action to that capitalized entity, the State. But I do mean that when the practical political situation called for universal military service in order to support and expand the existing state, the gospel of a Duty devoid of content naturally lent itself to the consecra-tion and idealization of such specific duties as the exist-ing national order might prescribe. The sense of duty must get its subject-matter somewhere, and unless sub-jectivism was to revert to anarchic or romantic individu-alism (which is hardly in the spirit of obedience to authoritative law) its appropriate subject-matter lies in the commands of a superior. Concretely what the State commands is the congenial outer filling of a purely inner sense of duty. That the despotism of Frederick the Great

* Bernhardi, "Germany and the Next War," pp. 63-64.

and of the Hohenzollerns who remained true to his policy
was at least that hitherto unknown thing, an enlightened
despotism, made the identification easier. Individuals
have at all times, in epochs of stress, offered their supreme sacrifice to their country's good. In Germany this
sacrifice in times of peace as well as of war has been
systematically reinforced by an inner mystic sense of a
Duty elevating men to the plane of the universal and
eternal.

In short, the sublime gospel of duty has its defects.
Outside of the theological and the Kantian moral traditions, men have generally agreed that duties are relative
to ends. Not the obligation, but some purpose, some
good, which the fulfillment of duty realizes, is the principle of morals. The business of reason is to see that the
end, the good, for which one acts is a reasonable one—
that is to say, as wide and as equitable in its working
out as the situation permits. Morals which are based
upon consideration of good and evil consequences not
only allow, but imperiously demand the exercise of a
discriminating intelligence. A gospel of duty separated
from empirical purposes and results tends to gag intelligence. It substitutes for the work of reason displayed
in a wide and distributed survey of consequences in
order to determine where duty lies an inner consciousness, empty of content, which clothes with the form of
rationality the demands of existing social authorities. A
consciousness which is not based upon and checked by
consideration of actual results upon human welfare is

none the less socially irresponsible because labeled Reason.

Professor Eucken represents a type of idealistic philosophy which is hardly acceptable to strict Kantians. Yet only where the fundamental Kantian ideas were current would such ethical ideas as the following flourish:

"When justice is considered as a mere means of securing man's welfare, and is treated accordingly—whether it be the welfare of individuals or of society as a whole makes no essential difference—it loses all its characteristic features. No longer can it compel us to see life from its own standpoint; no longer can it change the existing condition of things; no longer can it sway our hearts with the force of a primitive passion, and oppose to all consideration of consequences an irresistible spiritual compulsion. It degenerates rather into the complaisant servant of utility; it adopts herself to her demands, and in so doing suffers inward annihilation. It can maintain itself only when it comes as a unique revelation of the Spiritual Life within our human world, as a lofty Presence transcending all considerations of expediency." *

Such writing is capable of arousing emotional reverberations in the breasts of many persons. But they are emotions which, if given headway, smother intelligence, and undermine its responsibility for promoting the actual goods of life. If justice loses all its characteristic features when regarded as a means (the word "mere" inserted before "means" speaks volumes) of the welfare of society as a whole, then there is no objective and responsible criterion for justice at all. A justice which, irrespective of the determination of social well-being, proclaims itself

* Eucken, "The Meaning and Value of Life," translated by Gibson, p. 104.

as an irresistible spiritual impulsion possessed of the force of a primitive passion, is nothing but a primitive passion clothed with a spiritual title so that it is protected from having to render an account of itself. During an ordinary course of things, it passes for but an emotional indulgence; in a time of stress and strain, it exhibits itself as surrender of intelligence to passion.

The passage (from Bernhardi) quoted earlier puts the German principle of duty in opposition to the French principle of rights—a favorite contrast in German thought. Men like Jeremy Bentham also found the Revolutionary Rights of Man doctrinaire and conducing to tyranny rather than to freedom. These Rights were *a priori*, like Duty, being derived from the supposed nature or essence of man, instead of being adopted as empirical expedients to further progress and happiness. But the conception of duty is one-sided, expressing command on one side and obedience on the other, while rights are at least reciprocal. Rights are social and sociable in accord with the spirit of French philosophy. Put in a less abstract form than the revolutionary theory stated them, they are things to be discussed and measured. They admit of more or less, of compromise and adjustment. So also does the characteristic moral contribution of English thought—intelligent self-interest. This is hardly an ultimate idea. But at least it evokes a picture of merchants bargaining, while the categorical imperative calls up the drill sergeant. Trafficking ethics, in which each gives up something which he wants to get something which he wants more, is not the noblest kind of morals, but at least it is socially responsible as far as it goes. "Give so that it may be given to you in return" has at least some tendency to bring men together; it promotes agreement. It requires deliberation and discussion. This is just what the authoritative voice of a superior will not tolerate; it is the one unforgiveable sin.

The morals of bargaining, exchange, the mutual satisfaction of wants may be outlived in some remote future, but up to the present they play an important part in life. To me there is something uncanny in the scorn which German ethics, in behalf of an unsullied moral idealism, pours upon a theory which takes cognizance of practical motives. In a highly esthetic people one might understand the display of contempt. But when an aggressive and commercial nation carries on commerce and war simply from the motive of obedience to duty, there is awakened an unpleasant suspicion of a suppressed "psychic complex." When Nietzsche says, "Man does not desire happiness; only the Englishman does that," we laugh at the fair hit. But persons who profess no regard for happiness as a test of action have an unfortunate way of living up to their principle by making others *un*happy. I should entertain some suspicion of the complete sincerity of those who profess disregard for their own happiness, but I should be quite certain of their sincerity when it comes to a question of *my* happiness.

Within the Kantian philosophy of morals there is an idea which conducts necessarily to a philosophy of society and the State. Leibniz was the great German source of the philosophy of the enlightenment. Harmony was the dominant thought of this philosophy; the harmony of nature with itself and with intelligence; the harmony of nature with the moral ends of humanity. Although Kant was a true son of the enlightenment, his doctrine of the radically dual nature of the legislation of Reason put an end to its complacent optimism. According to Kant, morality is in no way a work of nature. It is the achievement of the self-conscious reason of man through the conquest of nature. The ideal of a final harmony remains, but it is an ideal to be won through a battle with the natural forces of man. His breach with the enlightenment is nowhere as marked as in his denial that man is by nature good. On the contrary, man is by nature evil—that is, his philosophical rendering of the doctrine of original sin. Not that the passions, appetites and senses are of themselves evil, but they tend to usurp the sovereignty of duty as the *motivating* force of human action. Hence morality is a ceaseless battle to transform all the natural desires of man into willing servants of the law and purpose of reason.

Even the kindly and sociable instincts of man, in which so many have sought the basis of both morality and organized society, fall under Kant's condemnation. As natural desires, they aspire to an illegitimate control in man's motives. They are parts of human self-love: the unlawful tendency to make happiness the controlling purpose of action. The natural relations of man to man are those of an unsocial sociableness. On the one hand, men are forced together by natural ties. Only in social relations can individuals develop their capacities. But no sooner do they come together than disintegrating tendencies set in. Union with his fellows give a stimulus to vanity, avarice and gaining power over others—traits which cannot show in themselves in individuals when they are isolated. This mutual antagonism is, however, more of a force in evolving man from savagery to civilization than are the kindly and sociable instincts.

"Without these unlovely qualities which set man over against man in strife, individuals would have lived on in perfect harmony, contentment and mutual love, with all their distinctive abilities latent and undeveloped."

In short, they would have remained in Rousseau's paradise of a state of nature, and

"perhaps Rousseau was right when he preferred the savage state to the state of civilization provided we leave out of account the last stage to which our species is yet destined to rise."

But since the condition of civilization is but an intermediary between the natural state and the truly or rational moral condition to which man is to rise, Rousseau was wrong.

"Thanks then be to nature for the unsociableness, the spiteful competition of vanity, the insatiate desires for power and gain."

These quotations, selected from Kant's little essay on an "Idea for a Universal History," are precious for understanding two of the most characteristic traits of subsequent German thought, the distinctions made between Society and the State and between Civilization and Culture. Much of the trouble which has been experienced in respect to the recent use of *Kultur* might have been allayed by a knowledge that *Kultur* has little in common with the English word "culture" save a likeness in sound. *Kultur* is sharply antithetical to civilization in its meaning. Civilization is a natural and largely unconscious or involuntary growth. It is, so to speak, a by-product of the needs engendered when people live close together. It is external, in short. Culture, on the other, is deliberate and conscious. It is a fruit not of men's natural motives, but of natural motives which have been transformed by the inner spirit. Kant made the distinction when he said that Rousseau was not so far wrong in preferring savagery to civilization, since civilization meant simply social decencies and elegancies and outward proprieties, while morality, that is, the rule of the end of Reason, is necessary to culture. And the real significance of the term "culture" becomes more obvious when he adds that it involves the slow toil of education of the Inner Life, and that the attainment of culture on the part of an individual depends upon long effort by the community to which he belongs. It is not primarily an individual trait or possession, but a conquest of the community won through devotion to "duty."

In recent German literature, Culture has been given even a more sharply technical distinction from Civilization and one which emphasizes even more its collective and nationalistic character. Civilization as external and uncontrolled by self-conscious purpose includes such things as language in its more spontaneous colloquial

expression, trade, conventional manners or etiquette, and
the police activities of government. *Kultur* comprises
language used for purposes of higher literature; commerce pursued not as means of enriching individuals but
as a condition of the development of national life; art,
philosophy (especially in that untranslatable thing, the
"Weltanschauung"); science, religion, and the activities
of the state in the nurture and expansion of the other
forms of national genius, that is, its activities in education and the army. The legislation of Bismarck with reference to certain Roman Catholic orders is nicknamed
Kultur-kampf, for it was conceived as embodying a
struggle between two radically different philosophies of
life, the Roman, or Italian, and the true Germanic, not
simply as a measure of political expediency. Thus it is
that a trading and military post like Kiao-Chou is offi-
cially spoken of as a "monument of Teutonic *Kultur*."
The war now raging is conceived of as an outer manifestation of a great spiritual struggle, in which what
is really at stake is the supreme value of the Germanic
attitude in philosophy, science and social questions generally, the "specifically German habits of feeling and
thinking."

Very similar motives are at work in the distinction
between society and the State, which is almost a commonplace of German thought. In English and American
writings the State is almost always used to denote society
in its more organized aspects, or it may be identified with
government as a special agency operating for the collective interests of men in association. But in German

literature society is a technical term and means something empirical and, so to speak, external; while the State, if not avowedly something mystic and transcendental, is at least a moral entity, the creation of self-conscious reason operating in behalf of the spiritual and ideal interests of its members. Its function is cultural, educative. Even when it intervenes in material interests, as it does in regulating lawsuits, poor laws, protective tariffs, etc., etc., its action has ultimately an ethical significance: its purpose is the furthering of an ideal community. The same thing is to be said of wars when they are really national wars, and not merely dynastic or accidental.

"Society" is an expression of man's egoistic nature; his natural seeking for personal advantage and profit. Its typical manifestation is in competitive economic struggle and in the struggle for honor and recognized social status. These have their proper place; but with respect even to them it is the duty of the State to intervene so that the struggle may contribute to ideal ends which alone are universal. Hence the significance of the force or power of the State. Unlike other forms of force, it has a sort of sacred import, for it represents force consecrated to the assertion and expansion of final goods which are spiritual, moral, rational. These absolute ends can be maintained only in struggle against man's individualistic ends. Conquest through conflict is the law of morals everywhere.

In Kant we find only the beginnings of this political philosophy. He is still held back by the individualism of the eighteenth century. Everything legal and political is conceived by him as external and hence outside the strictly moral realm of inner motivation. Yet he is not content to leave the State and its law as a wholly un-moral matter. The *natural* motives of man are, according to Kant (evidently following Hobbes), love of power, love of gain, love of glory. These motives are egoistic; they issue in strife—in the war of all against all. While such a state of affairs does not and cannot invade the inner realm of duty, the realm of the moral motive, it evidently presents a régime in which the conquest of the world of sense by the law of reason cannot be effected. Man in his rational or universal capacity must, there-fore, will an outward order of harmony in which it is at least possible for acts dictated by rational freedom to get a footing. Such an outer order is the State. Its province is not to promote moral freedom directly—only the moral will can do that. But its business is to hinder the hindrances to freedom: to establish a social condition of outward order in which truly moral acts may gradually evolve a kingdom of humanity. Thus while the State does not have a directly moral scope of action (since the coercion of motive is a moral absurdity), it does have a moral basis and an ultimate moral function.

It is the law of reason, "holy and inviolable," which impels man to the institution of the State, not natural sociability, much less considerations of expediency. And so necessary is the State to humanity's realization of its moral purpose that there can be no right of revolution. The overthrow and execution of the sovereign (Kant evidently had the French Revolution and Louis XVI in mind) is "an immortal and inexpiable sin like the sin against the Holy Ghost spoken of by theologians, which can never be forgiven in this world or in the next."

Kant was enough of a child of the eighteenth century to be cosmopolitan, not nationalistic, in his feeling. Since humanity as a whole, in its universality, alone truly corresponds to the universality of reason, he upheld the ideal of an ultimate republican federation of states; he was one of the first to proclaim the possibility of enduring peace among nations on the basis of such a federated union of mankind.

The threatened domination of Europe by Napoleon following on the wars waged by republican France put an end, however, to cosmopolitanism. Since Germany was the greatest sufferer from these wars, and since it was obvious that the lack of national unity, the division of Germany into a multitude of petty states, was the great source of her weakness; since it was equally obvious that Prussia, the one strong and centralized power among the German states, was the only thing which saved them all from national extinction, subsequent political philosophy in Germany rescued the idea of the State from the somewhat ambiguous moral position in which Kant had left it. Since a state which is an absolute moral necessity and whose actions are nevertheless lacking in inherent moral quantity is an anomaly, the doctrine almost calls for a theory which shall make the State the supreme moral entity.

Fichte marks the beginning of the transformation;

and, in his writings, it is easy to detect a marked difference of attitude toward the nationalistic state before and
after 1806, when in the battle of Jena Germany went
down to inglorious defeat. From the time of Fichte, the
German philosophy of the State blends with its philosophy of history, so that my reservation of the latter topic
for the next section is somewhat arbitrary, and I shall
not try rigidly to maintain the division of themes.

I have already mentioned the fact that Kant relaxes
the separation of the moral realm of freedom from the
sensuous realm of nature sufficiently to assert that the
former is *meant* to influence the latter and finally to
subjugate it. By means of the little crack thus introduced
into nature, Fichte rewrites the Kantian philosophy. The
world of sense must be regarded from the very start as
material which the free, rational, moral Ego has created
in order to have material for its own adequate realization of will. Fichte had a longing for an absolute unity
which did not afflict Kant, to whom, save for the con-
cession just referred to, a complete separation of the
two operations of legislative reason sufficed. Fichte was
also an ardently *active* soul, whose very temperament
assured him of the subordination of theoretical knowledge to moral action.

It would be as difficult to give, in short space, an adequate sketch of Fichte's philosophy as of Kant's. To
him, however, reason was the expression of the will, not
(as with Kant) the will an application of reason to action.
"Im Anfang war die That" is good Fichteanism. While
Kant continued the usual significance of the term Reason

(with only such modifications as the rationalism of his century had made current), Fichte began the transformation which consummated in later German idealism. If the world of nature and of human relations is an expression of reason, then reason must be the sort of thing, and have the sort of attributes by means of which the world must be construed, no matter how far away this conception of reason takes us from the usual meaning of the term. To Fichte the formula which best described such aspects of the world and of life as he was interested in was effort at self-realization through struggle with difficulties and overcoming opposition. Hence his formula for reason was a Will which, having "posited" itself, then "posited" its antithesis in order, through further action subjugating this opposite, to conquer its own freedom.

The doctrine of the primacy of the Deed, and of the Duty to achieve freedom through moral self-assertion against obstacles (which, after all, are there only to further this self-assertion) was one which could, with more or less plausibility, be derived from Kant. More to our present point, it was a doctrine which could be preached with noble moral fervor in connection with the difficulties and needs of a divided and conquered Germany. Fichte saw himself as the continuator of the work of Luther and Kant. His final "science of knowledge" brought the German people alone of the peoples of the world into the possession of the idea and ideal of absolute freedom. Hence the peculiar destiny of the German scholar and the German State. It was the duty and mission of German science and philosophy to contribute to the cause of the spiritual emancipation of humanity. Kant had already taught that the acts of men were to become gradually permeated by a spirit of rationality till there should be an equation of inner freedom of mind and outer freedom of action. Fichte's doctrine demanded an acceleration of the process. Men who have attained to a consciousness of the absolute freedom and self-activity must necessarily desire to see around them similar free beings. The scholar who is truly a scholar not merely knows, but he knows the nature of knowledge—its place and function as a manifestation of the Absolute. Hence he is, in a peculiar sense, the direct manifestation of God in the world—the true priest. And his priestly function consists in bringing other men to recognize moral freedom in its creative operation. Such is the dignity of education as conducted by those who have attained true philosophic insight.

Fichte made a specific application of this idea to his own country and time. The humiliating condition of contemporary Germany was due to the prevalence of egoism, selfishness and particularism: to the fact that men had lowered themselves to the plane of sensuous life. The fall was the worse because the Germans, more than any other people, were by nature and history conscious of the ideal and spiritual principle, the principle of freedom, lying at the very basis of all things. The key to the political regeneration of Germany was to be found in a moral and spiritual regeneration effected by means of education. The key, amid political division, to political unity was to be sought in devotion to moral unity. In this spirit Fichte preached his "Addresses to the German Nation." In this spirit he collaborated in the foundation of the University of Berlin, and zealously promoted all the educational reforms introduced by Stein and Humboldt into Prussian life.

The conception of the State as an essential moral Being charged with an indispensable moral function lay close to these ideas. Education is *the* means of the advancement of humanity toward realization of its divine perfection. Education is the work of the State. The syllogism completes itself. But in order that the State may carry on its educational or moral mission it must not only possess organization and commensurate power, but it must also control the conditions which secure the possibility offered to the individuals composing it. To adopt Aristotle's phrase, men must live before they can live nobly. The primary condition of a secure life is that everyone be able to live by his own labor. Without this, moral self-determination is a mockery. The business of the State, outside of its educational mission, is concerned with property, and this business means insuring property to everyone as well as protecting him in what he already possesses. Moreover, property is not mere physical possession. It has a profound moral significance, for it means the subjugation of physical things to will. It is a necessary part of the realization of moral personality: the conquest of the non-ego by the ego. Since property does not mean mere appropriation, but is a right recognized and validated by society itself, property has a social basis and aim. It is an expression not of individual egotism but of the universal will. Hence it is essential to the very idea of property and of the State that all the members of society have an equal opportunity for property. Hence it is the duty of the State to secure to its every member the right to work and the reward of his work.

The outcome, as expressed in his essay on "The Closed Industrial State," is State Socialism, based on moral and idealistic grounds, not on economic considerations. In order that men may have a real opportunity to develop their moral personalities, their right to labor and to adequate living, in return for their labor, must be assured. This cannot happen in a competitive society. Industry must be completely regulated by the State if these indispensable rights to labor and resulting comfort and security of life as means to moral volition are to be achieved. But a state engaged in unrestricted foreign trade will leave its workingmen at the mercy of foreign conditions. It must therefore regulate or even eliminate foreign commerce so far as is necessary to secure its own citizens. The ultimate goal is a universal state as wide as humanity, and a state in which each individual will act freely, without state-secured rights and state-imposed obligations. But before this cosmopolitan and philosophically anarchic condition can be reached, we must pass through a period of the nationalistic closed state. Thus at the end a wide gulf separates Fichte from Kant. The moral individualism of the latter has become an ethical socialism. Only in and by means of a circle of egos or

personalities does a human being attain the moral reason
and freedom which Kant bestowed upon him as his birth-
right. Only through the educational activities of the State
and its complete regulation of the industrial activities
of its members does the potential moral freedom of individuals become an established reality.

If I have devoted so much space to Fichte it is not
because of his direct influence upon affairs or even upon
thought. He did not found a school. His system was at
once too personal and too formal. Nevertheless, he expressed ideas which, removed from their special context
in his system, were taken up into the thought of cultivated Germany. Heine, speaking of the vogue of systems
of thought, says with profound truth that "nations have
an instinctive presentiment of what they require to fulfill
their mission."

And Fichte's thought infiltrated through many crev-
ices. Rodbertus and Lasalle, the socialists, were, for example, profoundly affected by him. When the latter was
prosecuted in a criminal suit for his "Programme of
Workingmen," his reply was that his programme was a
distinctively philosophic utterance, and hence protected
by the constitutional provision for freedom of science
and its teaching. And this is his philosophy of the State:

"The State is the unity and coöperation of individuals in a
moral whole.... The ultimate and intrinsic end of the State
is, therefore, to further the positive unfolding, the progressive
development of human life. Its function is to work out the
true end of man; that is to say, the full degree of culture of
which human nature is capable."

And he quotes with approval the words:

"The concept of the State must be broadened so as to make the State the contrivance whereby all human virtue is to be realized to the full."

And if he differs from Fichte, it is but in the assertion that since the laboring class is the one to whom the need most directly appeals, it is workingmen who must take the lead in the development of the true functions of the State.

Pantheism is a philosophic nickname which should be sparingly employed; so also should the term Monism. To call Fichte's system an ethical pantheism and monism is not to say much that is enlightening. But with free interpretation, the designation may be highly significant in reference to the spiritual temper of the Germany of the first part of the nineteenth century. For it gives a key to the presentiment of what Germany needed to fulfill its mission.

It is a commonplace of German historians that its unity and expansion to a great state powerful externally, prosperous internally, was wrought, unlike that of any other people, from within outward. In Lange's words, "our national development started from the most ideal and approximated more and more to the real." Hegel and Heine agree that in Germany the French Revolution and the Napoleonic career were paralleled by a philosophic revolution and an intellectual empire. You recall the bitter word that, when Napoleon was finally conquered and Europe partitioned, to Germany was assigned the

kingdom of the clouds. But this aërial and tenuous kingdom became a mighty power, working with and in the
statesmen of Prussia and the scholars of Germany to
found a kingdom on the solid earth. Spiritual and ideal
Germany made common cause with realistic and practical Prussia. As says Von Sybel, the historian of the
"Founding of the German Empire":

"Germany had been ruined through its own disintegration
and had dragged Prussia with it into the abyss. It was well
known that the wild fancies of the Conqueror hovered about
the utter annihilation of Prussia; if this should take place,
then east as well as west of the Elbe, not only political independence, but every trace of a German spirit, the German
language and customs, German art and learning—everything
would be wiped out by the foreigners. But this fatal danger
was perceived just at the time when everybody had been looking up to Kant and Schiller, had been admiring Faust, the
world-embracing masterpiece of Goethe's, and had recognized
that Alexander von Humboldt's cosmological studies and Niebuhr's "Roman History" had created a new era in European
science and learning. In such intellectual attainments the
Germans felt that they were far superior to the vanquisher
of the world and his great nation; and so the political interests of Prussia and the salvation of the German nationality
exactly coincided. Schleiermacher's patriotic sermons, Fichte's
stirring addresses to the German people, Humboldt's glorious
founding of the Berlin University, served to augment the re-
sisting power of Prussia, while Scharnhorst's recruits and mi-
litia were devoted to the defense of German honor and German
customs. Everyone felt that German nationality was lost if
Prussia did not come to its rescue, and that, too, there was no
safety possible for Prussia unless all Germany was free.

"What a remarkable providence it was that brought together,
as in the Middle Ages, on this ancient colonial ground, a throng
of the most energetic men from all districts of Germany. For

neither Stein nor his follower, Hardenberg, nor the generals, Scharnhorst, Bluecher and Gneisenau, nor the authors, Niebuhr, Fichte and K. F. Eichorn, nor many others who might be mentioned, were born in Prussia; yet because their thoughts centered in Germany, they had become loyal Prussians. The name Germany had been blotted from the political map of Europe, but never had so many hearts thrilled at the thought of being German.

"Thus on the most eastern frontier of German life, in the midst of troubles which seemed hopeless, the idea of German unity, which had lain dormant for centuries, now sprang up in a new birth. At first this idea was held exclusively by the great men of the times and remained the invaluable possession of the cultivated classes; but once started it spread far and wide among the younger generation.... But it was easier to defeat Napoleon than to bend the German sentiments of dualism and individualism to the spirit of national unity."

What I have called the ethical pantheism and monistic idealism of Fichte (a type of philosophy reigning almost unchallenged in Germany till almost the middle of the century) was an effective weapon in fighting and winning this more difficult battle. In his volume on the "Romantic School in Germany," Brandes quotes from the diary of Hoffman a passage written in 1809.

"Seized by a strange fancy at the ball on the 6th, I imagine myself looking at my own Ego through a kaleidoscope. All the forms moving around me are Egos and annoy me by what they do and leave undone."

It is a temptation to find in this passage a symbol both of German philosophy and of the temper of Germany at the time. Its outer defeats, its weakness in the world of action, had developed an exasperated introspection.

This outer weakness, coinciding, as Von Sybel points out, with the bloom of Germany in art, science, history, philology and philosophy, made the Ego of Germany the noblest contemporary object of contemplation, yet one surrounded with other national Egos who offended by what they did and what they did not do. Patriotism, national feeling, national consciousness are common enough facts. But nowhere save in Germany, in the earlier nineteenth century, have these sentiments and impulses been transformed by deliberate nurture into a mystic cult. This was the time when the idea of the *Volks-seele*, the *Volks-geist*, was born; and the idea lost no time in becoming a fact. Not merely poetry was affected by it, but philology, history and jurisprudence. The so-called historic school is its offspring. The science of social psychology derives from it at one remove. The soul, however, needed a body, and (quite in accord with German idealism) it formed a body for itself—the German state as a unified Empire.

While the idealistic period came first, it is important to bear in mind the kind of idealism it was. At this point the pantheistic allusion becomes significant. The idealism in question was not an idealism of another world but of *this* world, and especially of the State. The embodiment of the divine and absolute will and ideal is the existing world of nature and of men. Especially is the human ego the authorized and creative agent of absolute purpose. The significance of German philosophy was precisely to make men aware of their nature and destiny as the direct and active representatives of absolute and creative purpose.

If I again quote Heine, it is because, with his contempt for technical philosophy, he had an intimate sense of its human meaning. Of German pantheistic idealism, he wrote in 1833 while it was still in its prime:

"God is identical with the world. . . . But he manifests himself most gloriously in man, who feels and thinks at the same time, who is capable of distinguishing his own individuality from objective nature, whose intellect already bears within itself the ideas that present themselves to him in the phenomenal world. In man Deity reaches self-consciousness, and this self-consciousness God again reveals through man. But this revelation does not take place in and through individual man, but in and through collective humanity . . . which comprehends and represents in idea and in reality the whole God-universe. . . . It is an error to suppose that this religion leads men to indifference. On the contrary, the consciousness of his divinity will inspire man with enthusiasm for its manifestation, and from this moment the really noble achievements of true heroism glorify the earth."

In one respect, Heine was a false prophet. He thought that this philosophy would in the end accrue to the profit of the radical, the republican and revolutionary party in Germany. The history of German liberalism is a complicated matter. Suffice it in general to say that the honey the libertarians hived was appropriated in the end by the party of authority. In Heine's assurance that these ideas would in due time issue in action he was profoundly right. His essay closes with burning words, from which I extract the following:

"It seems to me that a methodical people, such as we, must begin with the reformation, must then occupy themselves with systems of philosophy, and only after their completion pass to the political revolution. . . . Then will appear Kantians, as little tolerant of piety in the world of deeds as in the world of ideas, who will mercilessly upturn with sword and axe the soil of our European life to extirpate the last remnants of the past. Then will come upon the scene armed Fichteans, whose fanaticism of will is to be restrained neither by fear nor self-interest, for they live in the spirit. . . . Most of all to be feared would be the philosophers of nature,* were they actively to mingle. . . . For if the hand of the Kantian strikes with strong unerring blow; if the Fichtean courageously defies every danger, since for him danger has in reality no existence;—the Philosopher of Nature will be terrible in that he has allied himself with the primitive powers of nature, in that he can conjure up the domestic forces of old German pantheism; and having done so, aroused in him that ancient Germanic eagerness which combats for the joy of the combat itself. . . . Smile not at any counsel as at the counsel of a dreamer. . . . The thought precedes the deed as the lightning the thunder. . . . The hour will come, As on the steps of an amphitheater, the nations will group themselves around Germany to witness the terrible combat."

In my preoccupation with Heine, I seem to have wandered somewhat from our immediate topic: the connection of the idealistic philosophy with the development and organization of the national state of Germany. But the necessity of the organized State to care for the moral interests of mankind was an inherent part of Fichte's thought. At first, *what* state was a matter of indifference.

---

* He refers to the followers of Schelling, who as matter of fact had little vogue. But his words may not unjustly be transferred to the naturalistic schools, which have since affected German thought.

In fact his sympathies were largely French and republican. Before Jena, he writes:

"What is the nation for a truly civilized Christian European? In a general way, Europe itself. More particularly at any time the State which is at the head of civilization.... With this cosmopolitan sense, we can be tranquil before the vicissitudes and catastrophes of history."

In 1807 he writes:

"The distinction between Prussia and the rest of Germany is external, arbitrary and fortuitous. The distinction between Germany and the rest of Europe is founded in nature."

The seeming gulf between the two ideas is easily bridged. The "Addresses on the Fundamental Features of the Present Age" had taught that the end of humanity on earth is the establishment of a kingdom in which all relations of humanity are determined with freedom or according to Reason—according to Reason as conceived by the Fichtean formula. In his "Addresses to the German Nation," in 1807-08, the unique mission of Germany in the establishment of this kingdom is urged as a motive for securing national unity and the overthrow of the conqueror. The Germans are the sole people who recognize the principles of spiritual freedom, of freedom won by action in accord with reason. Faithfulness to this mission will "elevate the German name to that of the most glorious among all the peoples, making this Nation the regenerator and restorer of the world." He personifies their ancestors speaking to them, and saying: "We in our time saved Germany from the Roman World Em-

pire." But "yours is the greater fortune. You may establish once for all the Kingdom of the Spirit and of Reason,
bringing to naught corporeal might as the ruling thing
in the world." And this antithesis of the Germanic and
the Roman principles has become a commonplace in the
German imagination. Moreover, for Germany to win is
no selfish gain. It is an advantage to all nations. "The
great promise of a kingdom of right reason and truth on
earth must not become a vain and empty phantom; the
present iron age is but a transition to a better estate."
Hence the concluding words: "There is no middle road:
If you sink, so sinks humanity entire with you, without
hope of future restoration."

The premises of the historic syllogism are plain. First,
the German Luther who saved for mankind the principle
of spiritual freedom against Latin externalism; then
Kant and Fichte, who wrought out the principle into a
final philosophy of science, morals and the State; as
conclusion, the German nation organized in order to win
the world to recognition of the principle, and thereby to
establish the rule of freedom and science in humanity as
a whole. The Germans are patient; they have a long
memory. Ideas produced when Germany was divided and
broken were retained and cherished after it became a
unified State of supreme military power, and one yielding to no other people in industrial and commercial
prosperity. In the grosser sense of the words, Germany
has not held that might makes right. But it has been
instructed by a long line of philosophers that it is the
business of ideal right to gather might to itself in order

that it may cease to be merely ideal. The State represents exactly this incarnation of ideal law and right in effective might. The military arm is part of this moral embodiment. Let sentimentalists sing the praises of an ideal to which no actual force corresponds. Prussian faith in the reality and enforcement among men of the ideal is of a more solid character. As past history is the record of the gradual realization in the Germanic State of the divine idea, future history must uphold and expand what has been accomplished. Diplomacy is the veiled display of law-clothed with force in behalf of this realization, and war is its overt manifestation. That war demands self-sacrifice is but the more convincing proof of its profound morality. It is the final seal of devotion to the extension of the kingdom of the Absolute on earth.

For the philosophy stands or falls with the conception of an Absolute. Whether a philosophy of absolutes is theoretically sound or unsound is none of my present concern. But that philosophical absolutism may be practically as dangerous as matter of fact political absolutism history testifies. The situation puts in relief what finally is at issue between a theory which is pinned to a belief in an Absolute beyond history and behind experience, and one which is frankly experimental. For any philosophy which is not consistently experimental will always traffic in absolutes no matter in how disguised a form. In German political philosophy, the traffic is without mask.

III

THE GERMANIC

PHILOSOPHY OF HISTORY

The unity of the German people longed for and dreamed of after 1807 became an established fact through the war of 1870 with France. It is easy to assign symbolic significance to this fact. Ever since the time of the French Revolution—if not before—German thought has taken shape in conflict with ideas that were characteristically French and in sharp and conscious antithesis to them. Rousseau's deification of Nature was the occasion for the development of the conception of Culture. His condemnation of science and art as socially corrupting and socially divisive worked across the Rhine to produce the notion that science and art are the forces which moralize and unify humanity. The cosmopolitanism of the French Enlightenment was transformed by German thinkers into a self-conscious assertion of nationalism. The abstract Rights of Man of the French

Revolution were set in antithesis to the principle of the rights of the citizen secured to him solely by the power of the politically organized nation. The deliberate breach of the revolutionary philosophy with the past, the attempt (foreshadowed in the philosophy of Descartes) to make a *tabula rasa* of the fortuitous assemblage of traditions and institutions which history offers, in order to substitute a social structure built upon Reason, was envisaged as the *fons et origo* of all evil. That history is itself incarnate reason; that history is infinitely more rational than the formal abstracting and generalizing reason of individuals; that individual mind becomes rational only through the absorption and assimilation of the universal reason embodied in historic institutions and historic development, became the articles of faith of the German intellectual creed. It is hardly an exaggeration to say that for almost a century the characteristic philosophy of Germany has been a philosophy of history even when not such in apparent form.

Yet the meaning of this appeal to history is lost unless we bear in mind that the Enlightenment after all transmitted to Germany, from medieval thought, its foundation principle. The appeal was not from reason to experience, but from analytic thought (henceforth condemned to be merely "Understanding"—"*Verstand*") to an absolute and universal Reason (*Vernunft*) partially revealed in nature and more adequately manifested in human history as an organic process. Recourse to history was required because not of any empirical lessons it has to teach, nor yet because history bequeathes to us stubborn institutions which must be reckoned with, but because history is the dynamic and evolving realization of immanent reason. The contrast of the German attitude with that of Edmund Burke is instructive. The latter had the same profound hostility to cutting loose from the past. But his objection was not that the past is an embodiment of transcendent reason, but that its institutions are an "inheritance" bequeathed to us from the "collected wisdom" of our forefathers. The continuity of political life centers not about an inner evolving Idea, but about "our hearths, our sepulchers and our altars." He has the same suspicion of abstract rights of man. But his appeal is to experience and to practical consequences. Since "circumstances give in reality to every principle its distinguishing color and discriminating effect," there is no soundness in any principle when "it stands stripped of every relation in all the nakedness and solitude of metaphysical abstraction."

According to the German view, the English protested against the abstract character of the French doctrine of rights founded in natural reason because of its interference with empirically or historically established rights and privileges; while the Germans protested because they perceived in the Revolution a radical error as to the nature and work of reason. In point of fact, the Germans never made that break with tradition, political or religious, of which the French Revolution is an emphatic symbol. I have already referred to Kant's disposition to regard church dogmas (of which, as dogmas, he disapproved) as vehicles of eternal spiritual truths—husks to

preserve an inner grain. All of the great German ideal-
ists gave further expression to this disposition. To Hegel,
for example, the substance of the doctrines of Protestant
Christianity is identical with the truths of absolute philosophy, except that in religion they are expressed in a
form not adequate to their meaning, the form, namely,
of imaginative thought in which most men live. The disposition to philosophize Christianity is too widely shown
in Germany to be dismissed as a cowardly desire at
accommodation with things established. It shows rather
an intellectual piety among a people where abstract and
formal freedom of thought and conscience had been
achieved without a violent political upheaval. Hegel
finds that the characteristic weakness of Romance thought
was an inner split, an inability to reconcile the spiritual
and absolute essence of reality with which religion deals
with the detailed work of intelligence in science and
politics. The Germans, on the contrary, "were predestined to be the bearers of the Christian principle and to
carry out the Idea as the absolutely Rational end." They
accomplished this, not by a flight away from the secular
world, but by realizing that the Christian principle is in
itself that of the unity of the subjective and the objective,
the spiritual and the worldly. The "spirit finds the goal
of its struggle, its harmony, in that very sphere which it
made the object of its resistance,—it finds that secular
pursuits are a spiritual occupation";—a discovery,
surely, which unites simplicity with comprehensiveness
and one which does not lead to criticism of the secular
pursuits carried on. Whatever is to be said of this as

philosophy, it expresses, in a way, the quality of German life and thought. More than other countries, Germany has had the fortune to preserve as food for its imaginative life and as emotional sanction the great ideas of the past. It has carried over their reinforcement into the pursuit of science and into politics—into the very things which in other countries, notably in the Latin countries, have been used as weapons of attack upon tradition.

Political development tells a somewhat similar tale. The painful transition from feudalism to the modern era was, for the most part, accomplished recently in Germany, and accomplished under the guidance of established political authorities instead of by revolt against them. Under their supervision, and mainly at their initiative, Germany has passed in less than a century to the régime of modern capitalistic competitive enterprise, moderated by the State, out of the dominion of those local and guild restrictions which so long held economic activity in corporate bonds. The governing powers themselves secured to members of the State what seems, at least to Germans, to be a satisfying degree of political freedom. Along with this absence of internal disturbance and revolution, we must put the fact that every step in the development of Germany as a unified political power has been effected by war with some of the neighbors by which it is hemmed in. There stands the unfolding sequence: 1815 (not to go back to Frederick the Great), 1864, 1866, 1870. And the significant thing about these wars is not that external territory was annexed as their consequence, but the rebound of external struggle upon the achieving of internal unity. No wonder the German imagination has been impressed with the idea of an organic evolution from within, which takes the form of a unity achieved through conflict and the conquest of an opposing principle.

Such scattering comments as these prove nothing. But they suggest why German thought has been peculiarly sensitive to the idea of historic continuity; why it has been prone to seek for an original implicit essence which has progressively unfolded itself in a single development. It would take much more than an hour to give even a superficial account of the growth of the historical sciences and historic methods of Germany during the first half of the eighteenth century. It would involve an account of the creation of philology, and the philological methods which go by the name of higher criticism; of their extension to archeology; of the historic schools of jurisprudence and political economy, as well as of the ways in which such men as Niebuhr, Mommsen and Ranke remade the methods of studying the past. I can only say here that Germany developed such an effective historical technique that even mediocre men achieved respectable results; and, much more significantly, that when Taine made the remark (quoted earlier) that we owe to the Germany of the half century before 1830 all our distinctively modern ideas, his remarks apply above all to the disciplines concerned with the historical development of mankind.

The bases of this philosophy are already before us. Even in Kant we find the idea of a single continuous development of humanity, as a progress from a reign of natural instinct to a final freedom won through adherence to the law of reason. Fichte sketched the stages already traversed on this road and located the point at which mankind now stands. In his later writings, the significance of history as the realization of the absolute purpose is increasingly emphasized. History is the continuous life of a divine Ego by which it realizes in fact what it is in idea or destiny. Its phases are successive stages in the founding of the Kingdom of God on earth. It and it only is the revelation of the Absolute. Along with this growing deification of history is the increased significance attached to nationalism in general and the German nation in particular. The State is the concrete individual interposed between generic humanity and particular beings. In his words, the national folk is the channel of divine life as it pours into particular finite human beings. He says:

"While cosmopolitanism is the dominant will that the purpose of the existence of humanity be actually realized in humanity, patriotism is the will that this end be first realized in the particular nation to which we ourselves belong, and that this achievement *thence* spread over the entire race."

Since the State is an organ of divinity, patriotism is religion. As the Germans are the only truly religious people, they alone are truly capable of patriotism. Other peoples are products of external causes; they have no self-formed Self, but only an acquired self due to general convention. In Germany there is a self which is self-wrought and self-owned. The very fact that Germany for centuries has had no external unity proves that its selfhood is metaphysical, not a gift of circumstance. This conception of the German mission has been combined with a kind of anthropological metaphysics which has become the rage in Germany. The Germans alone of all existing European nations are a pure race. They alone have preserved unalloyed the original divine deposit. Language is the expression of the national soul, and only the Germans have kept their native speech in its purity. In like vein, Hegel attributes the inner disharmony characteristic of Romance peoples to the fact that they are of mixed Germanic and Latin blood. A purely artificial cult of race has so flourished in Germany that many social movements—like anti-Semitism—and some of Germany's political ambitions cannot be understood apart from the mystic identification of Race, Culture and the State. In the light of actual science, this is so mythological that the remark of an American periodical that race means a number of people reading the same newspapers is sober scientific fact compared with it.*

* Chamberlain, for example, holds that Jesus must have been of Teutonic birth—a perfect logical conclusion from the received philosophy of the State and religion. Quite aware that there is much Slav blood in northern Germany and Romance blood in southern Germany, he explains that while with other peoples crossing produces a mongrel race, the potency of the German blood is such that cross-breeding strengthens it. While at one time he explains the historic strength of the Jew on the ground that he has kept his race pure, another place he allows his indignation at the Jews to lead him to include them among the most mongrel of all peoples. To one thing he remains consistent: By the very essence of race, the Semites represent a metaphysical principle inherently hostile to the grand Germanic principle. It perhaps seems absurd to dignify the vagaries of this garrulous writer, but according to all report the volumes in which such expressions occur, "The Foundations of the Nineteenth Century," has had august approval and much vogue.

At the beginning of history Fichte placed an *"Urvolk."* His account of it seems an attempt to rationalize at one stroke the legends of the Golden Age, the Biblical account of man before the Fall and Rousseau's primitive "state of nature." The *Urvolk* lived in a paradise of innocence, a paradise without knowledge, labor or art. The philosophy which demands such a Folk is comparatively simple. Except as a manifestation of Absolute Reason, humanity could not exist at all. Yet in the first stage of the manifestation, Reason could not have been appropriated by the self-conscious effort of man. It existed without consciousness of itself, for it was given, not, like all true self-consciousness, won by morally creative struggle. Rational in substance, in form it was but feeling or instinct. In a sense, all subsequent history is but a return to this primitive condition. But "humanity must make the journey on its own feet; by its own strength it must bring itself back to that state in which it was once without its own coöperating labor. . . . If humanity does not recreate its own true being, it has no real life." While philosophy compels us to assume a Normal People who, by "the mere fact of their existence, without science and art, found themselves in a state of perfectly developed reason," there is no ground for not admitting the existence at the same time of "timid and rude earth-born savages." Thus the original state of humanity would have been one of the greatest possible inequality, being divided between the Normal Folk existing as a manifestation of Reason and the wild and savage races of barbarism.

In his later period of inflamed patriotism this innocuous speculation grew a sting. He had determined that the present age—the Europe of the Enlightenment and the French Revolution—is the age of liberation from the external authority in which Reason had presented itself in the second age. Hence it is inherently negative: "an age of absolute indifference toward the Truth, an age of entire and unrestrained licentiousness." But the further evolution of the Divine Idea demands a Folk which has retained the primitive principle of Reason, which may redeem, therefore, the corrupt and rebellious modes of humanity elsewhere existing. Since the Germans are this saving remnant, they are the *Urvolk*, the Normal Nation, of the modern period. From this point on, idealization of past Germanic history and appeal to the nation to realize its unique calling by victory over Napoleon blend.

The Fichtean scaffolding tumbled, but these ideas persisted. I doubt if it is possible to exaggerate the extent to which German history has been systematically idealized for the last hundred years. Technically speaking, the Romantic movement may have passed away and an age of scientific history dawned. Actually the detailed facts have been depicted by use of the palette of Romanticism. Space permits but one illustration which would be but a literary curiosity were it not fairly typical. Tacitus called his account of the northern barbarians Germania—an unfortunate title in view of later developments. The characteristics assigned by him to the German tribes are such as any anthropologist could duplicate from any warlike barbaric tribe. Yet over and over again these traits (which Tacitus idealized as Cooper, say, idealized the North American Indian traits) are made the basis of the philosophic history of the German people. The Germans, for example, had that psychological experience now known as mana, manitou, tabu, etc. They identified their gods, in Tacitus' phrase, with "that mystery which they perceive by experiencing sacred fear." This turns out to be the germinal deposit of spiritual-mindedness which later showed itself in Luther and in the peculiar genius of the Germans for religious experience.

The following words are from no less an authority than Pfleiderer:

"Cannot we recognize in this point that truly German characteristic of *Innerlichkeit* which scorns to fix for sensuous perception the divine something which makes itself felt in the depths of the sensitive soul, which scorns to drag down the sublime mystery of the unknowable to the vulgar distinctness of earthly things? The fact that the Germans attached but little importance to religious ceremonies accords with this view."

To others, this sense of mystery is a prophetic anticipation of the Kantian thing-in-itself.

A similar treatment has been accorded to the personal and voluntary bond by which individuals attached themselves to a chieftain. Thus early was marked out the fidelity or loyalty, *Treue*, which is uniquely Germanic—although some war-like tribes among our Indians carried the system still further. I can allow myself but one more example of the way in which the philosophic sophistica-

tion of history has worked. No historian can be unconscious of the extent to which European culture has been
genuinely European—the extent to which it derives itself
from a common heritage of the ancient world and the
extent to which intermixtures and borrowings of culture
have gone on ever since. As to Germany, however, these
obvious facts have to be accommodated to the doctrine
of an original racial deposit steadily evolving from
within.

The method is simple. As respects Germany, these
cultural borrowings and crosses represent the intrinsic
universality of its genius. Through this universality,
the German spirit finds itself at home everywhere.
Consequently, it consciously appropriates and assimi-
lates what other peoples have produced by a kind
of blind unconscious instinct. Thus it was German
thought which revealed the truth of Hellenic culture, and
rescued essential Christanity from its Romanized petri-
faction. The principle of Reason which French enlightenment laid hold of only in its negative and destructive
aspect, the German spirit grasped in its positive and
constructive form. Shakespeare happened to be born in
England, but only the Germans have apprehended him
in his spiritual universality so that he is now more their
own than he is England's—and so on. But with respect
to other peoples, similar borrowings reveal only their
lack of inner and essential selfhood. While Luther is universal because he is German, Shakespeare is universal
because he is not English.

I have intimated that Fichte's actual influence was

limited. But his basic ideas of the State and of history
were absorbed in the philosophy of Hegel, and Hegel
for a considerable period absolutely dominated German
thinking. To set forth the ground principles of his "absolute idealism" would be only to repeat what has already been said. Its chief difference, aside from Hegel's
encyclopedic knowledge, his greater concrete historic
interest and his more conservative temperament, is his
bottomless scorn for an Idea, an Absolute, which merely
ought to be and which is only going to be realized after a
period of time. "The Actual *is* the Rational and the Rational *is* the Actual"—and the actual means the actuat-
ing force and movement of things. It is customary to call
him an Idealist. In one sense of much abused terms, he
is the greatest realist known to philosophy. He might
be called a Brutalist. In the inquiry Bourdon carried on
in Germany a few years ago (published under the title
of the "German Enigma"), he records a conversation
with a German who deplores the tendency of the Germans to forsake the solid bone of things in behalf of a
romantic shadow. As against this he appeals to the realistic sense of Hegel, who, "in opposition to the idealism
which had lifted Germany on wings, arrayed and mar-
shaled the maxims of an unflinching realism. He had
formulæ for the justification of facts whatever they might
be. That which *is*, he would say, is reason realized. And
what did he teach? That the hour has sounded for the
third act in the drama of humanity, and that the German
opportunity is not far off. . . . I could show you through-

out the nineteenth century the torrent of political and social ideas which had their source here."

I have said that the essential points of the Fichtean philosophy of history were taken up into the Hegelian system. This assimilation involved, however, a rectification of an inconsistency between the earlier and the later moral theories of Fichte. In his earlier ethical writings, emphasis fell upon conscious moral personality—upon the deliberate identification by the individual will of its career and destiny with the purpose of the Absolute. In his later patriotic philosophy, he asserts that the organized nation is the channel by which a finite ego acquires moral personality, since the nation alone transmits to individuals the generic principle of God working in humanity. At the same time he appeals to the resolute will and consciously chosen self-sacrifice of individuals to overthrow the enemy and re-establish the Prussian state. When Hegel writes that victory has been obtained, the war of Independence has been successfully waged. The necessity of emphasizing individual self-assertion had given way to the need of subordinating the individual to the established state in order to check the disintegrating tendencies of liberalism.

Haym has said that Hegel's "Philosophy of Law" had for its task the exhibition as the perfect work of Absolute Reason up to date of the "practical and political condition existing in Prussia in 1821." This was meant as a hostile attack. But Hegel himself should have been the last to object. With his scorn for an Ideal so impotent that its realization must depend upon the effort of private selves, an Absolute so inconsequential that it must wait upon the accidents of future time for manifestation, he sticks in politics more than elsewhere to the conviction that the actual *is* the rational. "The task of philosophy is to comprehend that which is, for that which is, is Reason." Alleged philosophies which try to tell what the State should be or even what a state ought in the future to come to be, are idle fantasies. Such attempts come too late. Human wisdom is like the bird of Minerva which takes its flight only at the close of day." * It comes, after the issue, to acknowledge what has happened. "The State is the rational in itself and for itself. Its substantial unity is an absolute end in itself. To it belongs supreme right in respect to individuals whose first duty is—just to be members of the State." . . . The State "is the absolute reality and the individual himself has objective existence, truth and morality only in his capacity as a member of the State." It is a commonplace of idealistic theism that nature is a manifestation of God. But Hegel says that nature is only an externalized, unconscious and so incomplete expression. The State has more, not less, objective reality than physical nature, for it is a realization of Absolute spirit in the realm of consciousness. The doctrine presents an extreme form of the idea, not of the divine right of kings, but of the divine right of States. "The march of God in history is the cause of the existence of states; their foundation is the power of

* Marx said of the historic schools of politics, law and economics that to them, as Jehovah to Moses on Mt. Sinai, the divine showed but its posterior side.

reason realizing itself as will. Every state, whatever it be, participates in the divine essence. The State is not the work of human art; only Reason could produce it." The State is God on earth.

His depreciation of the individual as an individual appears in every theme of his Philosophy of Right and History. At first sight, his theory of great world heroes seems inconsistent with his disregard of individuals. While the morality of most men consists simply in assimilating into their own habits the customs already found in the institutions about them, great men initiate new historic epochs. They derive "their purposes and their calling not from the calm regular course of things sanctioned by the existing order, but from a concealed fount, from that inner spirit hidden beneath the surface, which, striking the outer world as a shell, bursts it to pieces." The heroes are thus the exception which proves the rule. They are world characters; while they seem to be seeking personal interests they are really acting as organs of a universal will, of God in his further march. In his identification with the Absolute, the world-hero can have but one aim to which "he is devoted regardless of all else. Such men may even treat other great and sacred interests inconsiderately. . . . But so mighty a form must trample down many an innocent flower—crush to pieces many an object in its path." We are not surprised to see that Alexander, Cæsar and Napoleon are the characters he prefers to cite. One can only regret that he died before his contemplative piety could behold Bismarck.

A large part of the intellectual machinery by which

Hegel overcame the remnants of individualism found in prior philosophy came from the idea of organic development which had been active in German thought since the time of Herder. In his chief work ("Ideas for a Philosophy of the History of Humanity"), written in the closing decades of the eighteenth century, Herder holds that history is a progressive education of humanity. This idea, had from Lessing, is combined with the idea of Leibniz that change is evolution, by means of an internal force, of powers originally implicit in existence, and with the idea of Spinoza of an all-comprehensive substance. This idea of organic growth was then applied to language, literature and institutions. It soon obtained reinforcement from the rising science of biology. Long before the days of Darwin or Spencer, the idea of evolution had been a commonplace of German thought with respect to everything concerning the history of humanity. The notion was set in sharp antithesis to the conception of "making" or manufacturing institutions and constitutions, which was treated as one of the fallacies of the French philosophy of the Enlightenment. A combination of this notion of universal organic growth with the technique of prior idealism may fairly be said to have determined Hegel's whole philosophy. While Leibniz and Herder had emphasized the notion of harmony as an essential factor of the working of organic forces, Hegel took from Fichte the notion of a unity or synthesis arrived at by "positing," and overcoming an opposite. Struggle for existence (or realization) was thus an "organic" part of German thinking long before the teaching of Darwin, who, in fact, is usually treated by German writers as giving a rather superficial empirical expression to an idea which they had already grasped in its universal speculative form. It is characteristic of the extent in which Hegel thought in terms of struggle and overcoming that after stating why it was as yet impossible to include the Americas in his philosophy of history, and after saying that in the future the burden of world history will reveal itself there, he surmises that it may take the form of a "contest" between North and South America. No philosopher has ever thought so consistently and so wholly in terms of strife and overcoming as Hegel. When he says the "world history is the world judgment" he means judgment in the sense of assize, and judgment as victory of one and defeat of another—victory being the final proof that the world spirit has now passed from one nation to take up its residence in another. To be defeated in a way which causes the nation to take a secondary position among nations is a sign that divine judgment has been passed upon it. When a recent German writer argues that for Germany to surrender any territory which it has conquered during the present war would be sacrilegious, since it would be to refuse to acknowledge the workings of God in human history, he speaks quite in the Hegelian vein.

Although the phenomenon of nationalism was very recent when Hegel wrote, indeed practically contemporary with his own day, he writes in nationalistic terms the entire history of humanity. The State is the Individual of history; it is to history what a given man is to biography. History gives us the progressive realization or evolution of the Absolute, moving from one National Individual to another. It is law, the universal, which makes the State a State, for law is reason, not as mere subjective reflection, but in its manifestation as supreme over and in particulars. On this account, Hegel's statement that the fundamental principle of history is the progressive realization of freedom does not mean what an uninstructed English reader would naturally take it to mean. Freedom is always understood in terms of Reason. Its expression in history means that Thought has progressively become conscious of itself; that is, has made itself its own subject. Freedom is the *consciousness* of freedom. Liberty of action has little to do with it. Obviously it is only in the German idealistic system—particularly in the system of Hegel himself— that this has fully taken place. Meantime, when citizens of a state (especially of the state in which this philosophic insight has been achieved) take the laws of their state as their own ends and motives of action, they attain the best possible substitute for a reason which is its own object. They appropriate as their own personal reason the objective and absolute Reason embodied perforce in law and custom.

After this détour, we are led by Hegel to the fact that the Germans possess the greatest freedom yet attained by humanity, for the Prussian political organization most fully exemplifies Law, or the Universal, organizing under and within itself all particular arrangements of social and personal life. Some other peoples—particularly the Latin—have thought they could *make* constitutions, or at least that the form of their constitution was a matter of choice. But this is merely setting up the private conceit of individuals against the work of Absolute Reason, and thus marks the disintegration of a state rather than its existence. Other peoples have tried to found the government on the consent of the governed, unwitting of the fact that it is the government, the *specific* realization of Reason, which makes a state out of what is otherwise an anarchic mass of individuals. Other peoples have made a parliament or representative body the essential thing in government; in philosophic reality this is only a consultative body, having as its main function communication between classes (which are indispensable to an "organic" state) and the real government. The chief function of parliament is to give the opinion of the social classes an opportunity to feel it is being considered and to enable the real government to take advantage of whatever wisdom may chance to be expressed. Hegel seems quite prophetic when he says: "By virtue of this participation subjective liberty and conceit, with their general opinion, can show themselves palpably efficacious and enjoy the satisfaction of feeling themselves to count for something." Finally, the State becomes wholly and completely an organized Individual only in its external relations, its relations to other states. As his philosophy of history ignores the past in seizing upon the national state as the unit and focus of history, so it ignores all future possibility of a genuinely international federation to which isolated nationalism shall be subordinated. Bernhardi writes wholly in the Hegelian sense when he says that to expand the idea of the State into the idea of humanity is a Utopian error, for it would exclude the essential principle of life, struggle.

Philosophical justification of war follows inevitably from a philosophy of history composed in nationalistic terms. History is the movement, the march of God on earth through time. Only one nation at a time can be the latest and hence the fullest realization of God. The movement of God in history is thus particularly manifest in those changes by which unique place passes from one nation to another. War is the signally visible occurrence of such a flight of the divine spirit in its onward movement. The idea that friendly intercourse among all the peoples of the earth is a legitimate aim of human effort is in basic contradiction of such a philosophy. War is explicit realization of "dialectic," of the negation by which a higher synthesis of reason is assured. It effectively displays the "irony of the divine Idea." It is to national life what the winds are to the sea, "preserving mankind from the corruption engendered by immobility." War is the most effective preacher of the vanity of all merely finite interests; it puts an end to that selfish egoism of the individual by which he would claim his life and his property as his own or as his family's. International law is not properly law; it expresses simply certain usages which are accepted so long as they do not come into conflict with the purpose of a state—a purpose which always gives the supreme law of national life. Particularly against the absolute right of the "present bearer of the world spirit, the spirits of the other nations are absolutely without right. The latter, just like the nations whose epochs have passed, count no longer in universal history." Since they are already passed over from the standpoint of the divine idea, war can do no more than exhibit the fact that their day has come and gone. World history is the world's judgment seat.

For a period Hegelian thought was almost supreme in Germany. Then its rule passed away almost as rapidly as it had been achieved. After various shiftings, the trend of philosophic thought was definitely "Back to Kant." Kant's greater sobriety, the sharp distinction he drew between the realm of phenomena and science and the ideal noumenal world, commended him after the unbridled pretensions of Hegelian absolutism. For more than a generation Hegel was spoken of with almost universal contempt. Nevertheless his ideas, loosed from the technical apparatus with which he surrounded them, persisted. Upon the historical disciplines his influence was peculiarly deep and abiding. He fixed the ideas of Fichte and fastened them together with the pin of evolution. Since his day, histories of philosophy, or religion, or institutions have all been treated as developments through necessary stages of an inner implicit idea or purpose according to an indwelling law. And the idea of a peculiar mission and destiny of German history has lost nothing in the operation. Expressions which a bewildered world has sought since the beginning of the war to explain through the influence of a Darwinian struggle for

existence and survival of the fittest, or through the influence of a Nietzschean philosophy of power, have their
roots in the classic idealistic philosophy culminating in
Hegel.

Kant still remains the philosopher of Germany. The
division of life between the world of sense and of
mechanism and the world of the supersensible and purpose, the world of necessity and the world of freedom,
is more congenial than a complete monism. The attempts
of his successors to bridge the gap and set up a wholly
unified philosophy failed, historically speaking. But,
nevertheless, they contributed an indispensable ingredi-
ent to the contemporary German spirit; they helped
people the Kantian void of the supersensible with the
substantial figures of the State and its Historical Evolution and Mission. Kant bequeathed to the world an intellect devoted to the congenial task of discovering
causal law in external nature, and an inner intuition
which, in spite of its sublimity, had nothing to look at
except the bare form of an empty law of duty. Kant was
kept busy in proving the existence of this supernal but
empty region. Consequently he was not troubled by being
obliged to engage in the unremunerative task of spend-
ing his time gazing into a blank void. His successors
were not so fortunate. The existence of his ideal realm
in which reason, purpose and freedom are one was axio-
matic to them; they could no longer busy themselves with
proving its existence. Some of them, called the Roman-
ticists, filled it with visions, more or less poetic, which
frankly drew their substance from an imagination in-

flamed by emotional aspiration in revolt at the limitations of outward action. Others, called the idealistic philosophers, filled in the void, dark because of excess of light, with less ghostly forms of Law and the unfolding in History of Absolute Value and Purpose. The two worlds of Kant were too far away from each other. The later idealistic world constructions crumbled; but their débris supplied material with which to fill in the middle regions between the Kantian worlds of sense and of reason. This, I repeat, is their lasting contribution to present German culture. Where Kantianism has not received a filling in from the philosophy of history and the State, it has remained in Germany, as elsewhere, a critique of the methodology of science; its importance has been professional rather than human.

In the first lecture we set out with the suggestion of an inquiry into the influence of general ideas upon practical affairs, upon those larger practical affairs called politics. We appear to have concluded with a conviction that (in the instance before us at least) politics has rather been the controlling factor in the formation of philosophic ideas and in deciding their vogue. Yet we are well within limits when we say that ideas which were evoked ·in correspondence with concrete social conditions served to articulate and consolidate the latter. Even if we went so far as to say that reigning philosophies simply reflect as in a mirror contemporary social struggles, we should have to add that seeing one's self in a mirror is a definite practical aid in carrying on one's undertaking to its completion.

When what a people sees in its intellectual looking glass is its own organization and its own historic evolution as an organic instrument of the accomplishment of an Absolute Will and Law, the articulating and consolidating efficacy of the reflection is immensely intensified. Outside of Germany, the career of the German idealistic philosophy has been mainly professional and literary. It has exercised considerable influence upon the teaching of philosophy in France, England and this country. Beyond professorial circles, its influence has been considerable in theological directions. Without doubt, it has modulated for many persons the transition from a supernatural to a spiritual religion; it has enabled them to give up historical and miraculous elements as indifferent accretions and to retain the moral substance and emotional values of Christianity. But the Germans are quite right in feeling that only in Germany is this form of idealistic thinking both indigenous and widely applied.

A crisis like the present forces upon thoughtful persons a consideration of the value for the general aims of civilization of a philosophy of the *a priori*, the Absolute, and of their immanent evolution through the medium of an experience which as just experience is only a superficial and negligible vehicle of transcendent Laws and Ends. It forces a consideration of what type of general ideas is available for the articulation and guidance of our own life in case we find ourselves looking upon the present world scene as an *a priori* and an absolutistic philosophy gone into bankruptcy.

In Europe, speaking generally, "Americanism" is a synonym for crude empiricism and a materialistic utilitarianism. It is no part of my present task to show how largely this accusation is due to misunderstanding. It is simpler to inquire how far the charge points to the problem which American life, and therefore philosophy in America, must meet. It is difficult to see how any *a priori* philosophy, or any systematic absolutism, is to get a footing among us, at least beyond narrow and professorial circles. Psychologists talk about learning by the method of trial and error or success. Our social organization commits us to this philosophy of life. Our working principle is to try: to find out by trying, and to measure the worth of the ideas and theories tried by the success with which they meet the test of application in practice. Concrete consequences rather than *a priori* rules supply our guiding principles. Hegel found it "superficial and absurd to regard as objects of choice" social constitutions; to him "they were necessary structures in the path of development." To us they are the cumulative result of a multitude of daily and ever-renewed choices.

That such an experimental philosophy of life means a dangerous experiment goes without saying. It permits, sooner or later it may require, every alleged sacrosanct principle to submit to ordeal by fire—to trial by service rendered. From the standpoint of *a priorism*, it is hopelessly anarchic; it is doomed, *a priori*, to failure. From its own standpoint, it is itself a theory to be tested by experience. Now experiments are of all kinds, varying from those generated by blind impulse and appetite to those guided by intelligently formed ideas. They are as diverse as the attempt of a savage to get rain by sprinkling water and scattering thistledown, and that control of electricity in the laboratory from which issue wireless telegraphy and rapid traction. Is it not likely that in this distinction we have the key to the failure or success of the experimental method generalized into a philosophy of life, that is to say, of social matters—the only application which procures complete generalization?

An experimental philosophy differs from empirical philosophy as empiricism has been previously formulated. Historical empiricisms have been stated in terms of precedents; their generalizations have been summaries of what has previously happened. The truth and falsity of these generalizations depended then upon the accuracy with which they catalogued, under appropriate heads, a multiplicity of past occurrences. They were perforce lacking in directive power except so far as the future might be a routine repetition of the past. In an experimental philosophy of life, the question of the past, of precedents, of origins, is quite subordinate to prevision, to guidance and control amid future possibilities. Consequences rather than antecedents measure the worth of theories. Any scheme or project may have a fair hearing provided it promise amelioration in the future; and no theory or standard is so sacred that it may be accepted simply on the basis of past performance.

But this difference between a radically experimental philosophy and an empiristic philosophy only emphasizes the demand for careful and comprehensive reflection with respect to the ideas which are to be tested in practice. If an *a priori* philosophy has worked at all in Germany it is because it has been based on an *a priori* social constitution—that is to say, on a state whose organization is such as to determine in advance the main activities of classes of individuals, and to utilize their particular activities by linking them up with one another in definite ways. It is a commonplace to say that Germany is a monument to what can be done by means of conscious method and organization. An experimental philosophy of life in order to succeed must not set less store upon methodic and organized intelligence, but more. We must learn from Germany what methodic and organized work means. But instead of confining intelligence to the technical means of realizing ends which are predetermined by the State (or by something called the historic Evolution of the Idea), intelligence must, with us, devote itself as well to construction of the ends to be acted upon.

The method of trial and error or success is likely, if not directed by a trained and informed imagination, to score an undue proportion of failures. There is no possibility of disguising the fact that an experimental philosophy of life means a hit-and-miss philosophy in the end. But it means missing rather than hitting, if the aiming is done in a happy-go-lucky way instead of by bringing to bear all the resources of inquiry upon locating the target, constructing propulsive machinery and figuring out the curve of trajectory. That this work is, after all, but hypothetical and tentative till it issue from thought into action does not mean that it might as well be random guesswork; it means that we can do still better next time if we are sufficiently attentive to the causes of success and failure this time.

America is too new to afford a foundation for an *a priori philosophy*; we have not the requisite background of law, institutions and achieved social organization. America is too new to render congenial to our imagination an evolutionary philosophy of the German type. For our history is too obviously future. Our country is too big and too unformed, however, to enable us to trust to an empirical philosophy of muddling along, patching up here and there some old piece of machinery which has broken down by reason of its antiquity. We must have system, constructive method, springing from a widely inventive imagination, a method checked up at each turn by results achieved. We have said long enough that America means opportunity; we must now begin to ask: Opportunity for what, and how shall the opportunity be achieved? I can but think that the present European situation forces home upon us the need for constructive planning. I can but think that while it gives no reason for supposing that creative power attaches *ex officio* to general ideas, it does encourage us to believe that a philosophy which should articulate and consolidate the ideas to which our social practice commits us would clarify and guide our future endeavor.

Time permits of but one illustration. The present situation presents the spectacle of the breakdown of the whole philosophy of Nationalism, political, racial and cultural. It is by the accident of position rather than any virtue of our own that we are not sharers in the present demonstration of failure. We have borrowed the older philosophy of isolated national sovereignty and have lived upon it in a more or less half-hearted way. In our internal constitution we are actually interracial and international. It remains to see whether we have the courage to face this fact and the wisdom to think out the plan of action which it indicates. Arbitration treaties, international judicial councils, schemes of international disarmament, peace funds and peace movements, are all well in their way. But the situation calls for more radical thinking than that which terminates in such proposals. We have to recognize that furtherance of the depth and width of human intercourse is the measure of civilization; and we have to apply this fact without as well as within our national life. We must make the accident of our internal composition into an idea, an idea upon which we may conduct our foreign as well as our domestic policy. An international judicial tribunal will break in the end upon the principle of national sovereignty.

We have no right to cast stones at any warring nation till we have asked ourselves whether we are willing to forego this principle and to submit affairs which limited imagination and sense have led us to consider strictly national to an international legislature. In and of itself, the idea of peace is a negative idea; it is a police idea. There *are* things more important than keeping one's body whole and one's property intact. Disturbing the peace is bad, not because peace is disturbed, but because the fruitful processes of coöperation in the great experiment of living together are disturbed. It is futile to work for the negative end of peace unless we are committed to the positive idea which it cloaks: Promoting the efficacy of human intercourse irrespective of class, racial, geographical and national limits. Any philosophy which should penetrate and particulate our present social practice would find at work the forces which unify human intercourse. An intelligent and courageous philosophy of practice would devise means by which the operation of these forces would be extended and assured in the future. An American philosophy of history must perforce be a philosophy for its future, a future in which freedom and fullness of human companionship is the aim, and intelligent coöperative experimentation the method.

THE END

INDEX